Lists of Germans
From The Palatinate
Who Came to England in 1709

Compiled by

JOHN TRIBBEKO and GEORGE RUPERTI

Reprinted from

THE NEW YORK GENEALOGICAL
AND BIOGRAPHICAL RECORD

CLEARFIELD

Excerpted and Reprinted from

The New York Genealogical and Biographical Record

Volumes XL and XLI

1909-1910

Reprinted for
Clearfield Company, Inc. by
Genealogical Publishing Co., Inc.
Baltimore, Maryland
1990, 1994, 1996, 1998, 2003

Library of Congress Catalogue Card Number 65-29270
International Standard Book Number: 0-8063-0329-8

Made in the United States of America

INDEX TO

BOARD OF TRADE LISTS

LISTS OF GERMANS FROM THE PALATINATE WHO CAME TO ENGLAND IN 1709.

The following lists are copied from the original documents preserved in the British Museum Library, London, England, and should be of the greatest genealogical interest to those families in the States of New York, New Jersey, Pennsylvania and elsewhere, which claim descent from the so-called Palatine settlers. These lists have never before been printed to the knowledge of the Editor, and it should be noted that the word "son" or "sons" and "dau." or "daus." followed by figures denote that the heads of the family had as many sons or daughters, as there are figures, and that these sons and daughters were of the respective ages denoted by the figures. The word "wife" indicates that the head of the family was married and that the wife was living. The abbreviations "Ref.," "Luth.," "Bap." and "Cath.," mean that the family belonged to the Reformed, Lutheran, Baptist or Catholic Churches.

BOARD OF TRADE MISCELLANEOUS. VOL. 2 D. 57.

A list of all the poor Germans lately come over from the Palatinate into this kingdom taken in St. Catharine's the sixth May, 1709.

FIRST ARRIVALS.

NAME	AGE	WIFE	SONS	DAUS.	CHURCH
Turch, Caspar, student of Divinity..............	25	sing.			Ref.
Machtig,Jacob,Schoolmaster	40	wife	11, 6	13, 12	"
HUSBANDMEN & VINEDRESSERS					
Meningen, John...........	40	wife	5, 2		Ref.
Faubell, John.............	30	"		1½	Luth.
Leibengut, John Wendell...	53	none	28		Ref.
Ends, Matthew	50	wife	20		"
Engelsbruecher, Nicol......	57	"		15	"
Hirtzbach, Anton..........	36	"	10, 8, 5	4	"
Rohrbach, Christian........	34	"		¼	"
Hubmacher, Niclas........	33	"	6	4, 1	"
Bollon, Cristoff............	26	"	4	2, ½	"
Meyer, Henry.............	41	"		8, ½	"
Hobler, Abraham (he is also a tailor)............	32	"	6	1	"
Dixion, David (Englishman)	40	"	10		"
Kaff, Bazar..............	38	"	14, 12, ¼		Cath.
Lauber, Jacob.............	37	"		7, 6, 2	Ref.
Garrinot, Peter............	37	"			Cath.
Haun, Andrew............	50	"	17, 11, 11, 8, 4	19. 14	Luth.
Kliein, Michael............	28	"		6, ½	"
Presler, Valentine..........	40	"	6, 4, 1½	10, 8	Cath.
Mey, David...............	24	"			Ref.
Wagner, John.............	43	"	10, 8	12, 5, 3	"
Hornigh, John George......	38	"	8, 2	12, 10	"

NAME	AGE	WIFE	SONS	DAUS.	CHURCH
Albrecht, James............	26	wife			Luth.
Erkel, Bernhard............	33	"			Ref.
Hirzeach, Martin...	56	"	24, 14	21, 18	"
Bahr, John................	38	"	8, 6, 3		"
Shwartz, Matthias........ ..	33	"	11, 4	8	Luth.
Durk, John Adam..........	36	"	10	12, 2	Cath.
Shonweiss, John............	48	"	1½	14, 12	Ref.
Ebert, Hartman............	30	"			"
Herman, Valentine.........	34	"	7½		Luth.
Helffert, Peter.............	49	"			Ref.
Gnaedi, Benedict...........	60	"	24	25	"
Gerhard, John George......	41	"	12, 2	16, 14, 8, 6	"
Kueffer, John..............	36	"		3, 1	
Smith, John...............	47	"	7, 5, 3, 1	24, 17, 15, 13, 11, 9	Luth.
Frey, Conrad..............	61	"	17, 14	25, 19	
Shwa, Peter (also a cooper).	33	"	1	1½	Luth.
Seibert, Conrad............	31	"	4	1½	Ref.
Wenig, Peter..............	26	"		1½	Luth.
am Thor, Conrad...........	30	"		1½	Ref.
Daun, George.............	35	"		2	"
Reuling, Jacob.............	28	"		1	Luth.
Schneider, John Michael....	24	"	10	1½	"
Vogt, Abraham............	50	"	12	16, 9, 7, 4	Ref.
Schneider, Philip...........	36	"	10, 3	¼	Cath.
Geisell, George............	42	"	6, 1		"
Klein, Peter...............	42	"	2½	¼	"
Smith, Jacob..............	51	"	14, 10	4	Luth.
Trombauer, Niclas.........	33	"	6	3, ¾	Cath.
Werner, Christoff..........	33	"	1		Luth.
Huebner, Anton............	30	"	5, ¾	2½	"
Heidman, Peter............	30	"		6, 2½, ¼	"
Thevoux, Daniel...........	44	"	6	8	Ref.
Nagel, John...............	40	"		9	"
Rath (Bath), John..........	29	"	2	6 da.	
Schmitzer, John Martin.....	26	"	1		Cath.
Berg, Frederick............	32	"	3	1	Luth.
Bolker, Charles............	25	"			Ref.
Herman, Peter.............	28	"	5, 2¾	1 mo.	"
Glaents, John..............	46	"	18		"
Klein, John Jacob..........	25	"	4		"
Messer, Sylvester..........	45	"	14, 5	23, 7	"
Schaeffer, Joseph..........	38	"	10, 3	14, 12, 8, 5	"
Meyer, Hartman...........	38	"	9	7, 4	"
Zeber, John...............	46	"	18, 4	11, 8	"
Daninger, Jacob...........	35	"	6, 1	10, 4	Luth.
Seibert, Martin............	35	"	2	4	Ref.
Bekell, Philip.............	53	"	10	12, 8, 6, 6, 1½	
Haas, John................	52	"	16, 11	9, 3	Ref.
Klein, John...............	55	"	14, 6		Cath.
Wayner, Henry............	40	"	8, 4	12	Luth.
Weitzell, John.............	29	"	1½, ¼		Luth.
Schwengel, John...........	40	"	12	4, 2, 1	"
Klug, George..............	37	"	1½		Ref.
Zeisler, Lorentz...........	40	"	6, 3	1	"
Klaemer, Ludwig..........	37	"	¾	6, 4	Luth.
Spuehler, Jacob............	30	"	1		Ref.
am Rheine, John...........	30	"			Cath.
Closterbeker, John........	31	"	6	4, 1	Luth.
Emichen, Ernst............	55	"	9, 6, 5, 1½		"

NAME	AGE	WIFE	SONS	DAUS.	CHURCH
Shwartze, John............	32	wife	1¾	7	R. f.
Hahrlaender, Conrad.......	30	"	4½, 3		Cath.
Kaldauer, Valentine........	34	"	6, 1	14, 9, 3	"
Kuhner, Jacob............	36	"	10, 8, 6	2	Luth.
Blesinger, Daniel..........	27	"		4, 1¼	
Lang, Philip..............	35	"	13	3	Cath.
Sheuer, John Adam........	35	"	8, 5	2	Ref.
Obender, Samuel..........	33	"		2	"
Hoffart, John Adam........	27	"			Luth.
Weinrich, Balzar..........	40	"	7, 5, 3	15	"
Fuhrman, Jacob...........	34	none		7, 5	Ref.
Hesse, John..............	40	wife		7, 4	"
Schletzer, Jeremy..........	53	"	7, 5	12, 9, ¼	Luth.
Drechsler, John Peter......	28	"	1		"
Herman, Daniel...........	28	"	2	4	Ref.
am Ende, John Philip......	35	"	¾	3	Luth.
Vogt, John...............	25	"	2		Ref.
Berstler, Adam............	30	"	8, 4	1	Luth.
Kolb, Henry..............	30	"		6, 3, ½	Bap.
Clemens, Gerhard (also a linen cloth weaver........	28	"	5, 1½		"
Volweider, Jacob...........	27	"			"
Baumann, Michael.........	37	"		8	Ref.
Herman, Jacob............	26	sing.			Luth.
Schaeffer, John Conrad.....	23	"			Ref.
Mueller, Valentine.........	23	"			"
Hassmer, John............	25	"			"
Bretschi, Lorentz..........	26	"			"
Hermann, Niclas..........	52	"			"
Rausch, George...........	24	"			Luth.
Rudolff, John.............	24	"			"
Kolb, Arnold.............	22	"			Bap.
Hocky, Peter.............	26	"			Ref.
Hocky, Andrew....	22	"			"
THESE ARE ONLY HUSBANDMEN					
Goebell, Paul.............	59	wife	23	25	Luth.
Gring, Jacob..............	26	"		1	Ref.
Jocobi, John Thomas.......	38	"	13, 9	1	Luth.
Zitel, Jacob..............	25	"			Ref.
Kinfeller, Frederick........	37	"	5	12	"
Becker, Gerhard (also a joiner).................	38	"	½	5	"
Notzel, Rudolf............	38	"		8, 7, 2	"
duBois, Abraham (tobacco planter)................	38	"	13, 9, 3	7	"
Durbecker, John Adam.....	26	"		2	"
Jalathe, John Wm.........	38	"	6, ½	12	"
Hartman, John George.....	40	"	9		Cath.
Buff, George..............	28	"		1	Luth.
Thomas, John George......	50	"	7, 2	5	"
Wismar, Jacob (also a tailor).	50	"	20	22	Bap.
Pfeiffer, John Jacob........	42	"	8	3	Ref.
Schuetz, John.............	46	"		6, 4, 3, 1½	"
Hubscher, Andrew.........	50	"	22	13, 9, 8, 5	Bap.
Trumph, John Michael.....	48	none	18		Ref.
le Dee, John.............	47	"		20, 16	"
le Fevre, Abram...........	50	wife	7	20	"
Schrager, Andrew..........	53	"		23, 20	Bap.
Oberholtzer, Mark........	45	"	10, 8, 3	6, 1	"

NAME	AGE	WIFE	SONS	DAUS.	CHURCH
Fodder, John.............	38	wife	9, 4	1	Ref.
Staehler, Peter............	24	sing.			"
Hermann, Niclas..........	52	"			"
Moor, John...............	25	"			"
Moor, Austin..............	22	"			"
Moor, John Wm...........	18				"
Pelle, Peter...............	24	"			"
Wentzen, Peter...	25	"			"
Hagder, John.............	27	"			"
Kuhlwein, Philip..........	26	"			"
HERDSMEN					
Beller, Jacob..............	28	wife	1½		Cath.
Zinkhan, Conrad..........	37	"	1¼	1¼, 4	Ref.
Schlingluff, John..........	30	"	20, 15, 11		"
WHEELWRIGHT					
Eyeach, John Valentine.....	22	sing.			Ref.
SMITHS					
Keyser, Geo. Frederick.....	40	wife		7, 5	Ref.
Zimmerman, John Wolff....	53	"	20, 16	22,18,11,9	Luth.
Willich, Peter.............	30	. "		5, 2	Ref.
Leucht, Lewis.............	54	"	22		Luth.
Andrew, Benedict..........	40	"	1½		"
Hebenstreit, John Jas. (lock-					
smith)..................	30	"			Ref.
Degen, Felix..............	23	sing.			"
Heffen, Bartin.............	30	"			"
Zeitz John Peter...........	30	"			
Bauer, George.............	40	"			Luth.
Gruendner, Matthew.......	33	"			Ref.
SADDLER					
Dieterich, John............	44	wife	2		Cath.
MILLERS					
Lup, Henry................	28	wife	11, 9, 6	8	Ref.
Guth, Henry..............	30	sing.			"
Rebell, Jacob..............	30	"			"
Escherich, John............	37	"			Luth.
Anke, Joseph..............	28	"			Ref.
BAKERS					
Muller, Daniel.............	50	sing.			Ref.
Penning, Daniel...........	22	"			Luth.
BREWER					
Truat, John...............	40	wife	10, 6		Ref.
BUTCHERS					
de Rochefort, Peter........	38	wife	12, 10	15, 3	Ref.
Smith, Henry..............	53	"	22,19,12, 6	15	Luth.
Buehler, John.............	48	"		16, 12, 11	"
CLOTH & LINEN WEAVERS					
Walter, John George.......	45	wife	12, 9, ½	17, 7	Ref.
Rider, Niclas..............	38	"			"
Lucas, Francis.............	46	"	17, 11	19,8,6,3,3	"
Bruchly, John Henry.......	32	"	4, 2		"
Adeler, Henry.............	41	"	12		"

NAME	AGE	WIFE	SONS	DAUS.	CHURCH·
Hoherluth, George Adam...	45	wife	12, 9	17, 14	Bap.
Ziegler, Michael..........	25	sing.			Luth.
Bien, John...............	24	"			Bap.
TAILORS					
Boos, John Henry..........	22	wife			Ref.
Riedell, John George.......	30	"	1	6	Luth.
Koenig, John Adam........	30	sing.			"
SHOEMAKER					
Mueller, John Jacob........	42	wife	13, 12, 10, 8, 6, 4	15	Ref.
Hohenstein, Christian......	37	"	4, 1	6	Cath.
Schlottenhofer, Christof.....	38	"	6, 1		Ref.
Galathe, John Jacob........	32	"	12	6	"
Mendon, Jacob.............	22	sing.			"
STOCKING WEAVER					
Mason, Niclas.............	46	wife	17		Ref.
TANNER					
Bergleuchter, Anton........	24	sing.			Ref.
CARPENTERS					
Guthzeit, William..........	29	wife	3	2	Luth.
Neidhofer, John Quirinus...	42	"	8	20, 17	"
Gessienger, Henry..........	28	"		½	"
Weber, John Engel........	46	"		20, 18, 13, 8, 4	"
Weber, John Jacob.........	26	"			"
Schaeffer, John.............	44	"	14, 10, 2, 5 da.	8, 5	Ref.
Bauer, Christian...........	30	"	8, 6	10, 4, 1	"
Galathe, Jacob.............	75	sing.			"
JOINERS					
Heyde, Peter..............	28	wife	1½		Ref.
Hagenbeck, frederick......	30	"	6, 3		Cath.
Kirchofen, Francis Ludwig..	37	sing.			Ref.
MASONS					
Schaeffer, John.............	26	wife	1		Ref.
Hakl, John George........	30	"	1	9, 5, 4	Cath.
COOPERS					
Stutz, John Eberhard.......	44	wife	7, 2	5	Luth.
Henrich, Lorentz..........	48	"	2½	1¼	Ref.
Reiser, John Peter.........	40	"	14, 12, 8, 6, 1½		Cath.
BOOKBINDER					
Hoffstaetter, Philip........	19	sing.			Ref.
MINER					
la Forge, John Wm..... ...	50	wife			Ref.
UNMARRIED PERSONS, WIDOWS, ETC.					
Rose, Anna...............	53		9	17, 4	Ref.
Rose, Catherine...........	24			15	"
Bettinger, Anna Christina...	60				"

NAME	AGE	WIFE	SONS	DAUS.	CHURCH
Tanner, Cathrina...........	35			6	Cath.
Schoen, Maria Cathrina.....	38		10, 8, 4	1 ½	"
Winter, Maria Cathrina.....	50			20	"
Raths, Jane................	50				Ref.
Schwaegerin, Apollonia.....	50				"
Martins, Gertrud...........	42		9		
Eschelmanns, Anna........	37		16		Bap.
George Riedel's mother-in-law....................	50				Luth.
Warambour, Mary........	56		24, 23, 19, 17	22	Ref.
UNMARRIED					
Sister of Henry Meyers.....	42				Ref.
Sister-in-law of Michael Klein	20				"
Cathrina, Servant maid.....	36				"
Friede, Cathrina...........	30				"
Wagner, Mary Elizabeth...	24				
Bauer, Christina...........	23				Bap.

SUCH AS ENTERED THEIR NAMES LAST.

NO. OF THE FAMILY	NAME
4	Lang, Johan
5	Stutz, Eberhard
4	Pens, Benedict
1	Bohm, Johannes
1	Denias, Philip
1	Albenz, Christoph
1	Lichtneggar, Gottlob August
1	Graeff, Jacob, whose parents live in Pennsylvania, a boy 10 years of age
1	George Klug, his sister's son, a boy 15 years of age

19   Persons who entered their names last

ALL PAGES SUMMED UP.

Husbandmen & Vinedressers....	115	Tailors.......................	3
Only Husbandmen..............	32	Shoemakers...................	5
Herdsmen.....................	3	Stocking Weaver..............	1
Wheelwright....................	1	Tanner.......................	1
Smiths.........................	11	Carpenters...................	8
Saddler.......................	1	Joiners	3
Millers........................	5	Masons.......................	2
Bakers.........................	2	Coopers......................	3
Brewer........................	1	Bookbinder...................	1
Butchers.......................	3	Miner........................	1
Cloth & Linen Weavers........	8		

The whole sum of men, wives and children, lately come over from the Palatinate into this Kingdom makes out 852.

JOHN TRIBBEKO,
    Chaplain to his late Royal
    Highness Prince George
    of Denmark.

GEORGE ANDREW RUPERTI,
    Minister of the German Lutheran
    Church in the Savoye.

Endorsed: Miscellaneous. Account of the number, conditions and trades of the poor German come over from the Palatinate.

Referred to in mem. from the Lutheran minister.

Received and read 12th May, 1709, D.57 Entered A folio 401.

LISTS OF GERMANS FROM THE PALATINATE WHO CAME TO ENGLAND IN 1709.

The following lists are copied from the original documents preserved in the British Museum Library, London, England, and should be of the greatest genealogical interest to those families in the States of New York, New Jersey, Pennsylvania and elsewhere, which claim descent from the so-called Palatine settlers. These lists have never before been printed to the knowledge of the Editor, and it should be noted that the word "son" or "sons" and "dau." or "daus." followed by figures denote that the heads of the family had as many sons or daughters, as there are figures, and that these sons and daughters were of the respective ages denoted by the figures. The word "wife" indicates that the head of the family was married and that the wife was living. The abbreviations "Ref.," "Luth.," "Bap." and "Cath.," mean that the family belonged to the Reformed, Lutheran, Baptist or Catholic Churches.

BOARD OF TRADE MISCELLANEOUS. VOL. 2 D. 64.

The second list of 1193 Palatines lately come over from Germany into this kingdom taken at Walworth, 27th of May, 1709, by Mr. John Tribbeko and Mr. Ruperti, German Ministers.

SECOND ARRIVALS.

NAME	AGE	WIFE	SONS	DAUS.	CHURCH
SCHOOLMASTERS.					
Schenne, Justus............	34	wife	4, 1¼		Luth.
Moritz, John Philip........	50	"		25, 27	Ref.
Rinner, Hans Henrich......	45	"	20, 4	14, 11, 9, 5	"
HUSBANDMEN & VINEDRESSERS					
Hodell, Michael............	34	wife		6, 3	Ref.
Schmidt, John George......	30	"	4	2	"
Hach, John Peter..........	60		20		"
Hach, John.	30	wife	14		"
Schmidt, Frederick........	30	"	4		Luth.
Conradt, Martin...........	45	"	9, 5	13, 3	"
Richardt, John............	46	"	14, 3	19, 12, 9, 6	Ref.
Bertram, Peter............	21	sing.			"
Korn, George.............	50	wife		7	Luth.
Dietrich, John Peter........	36	"	8	5, 1¼	"
Hertzog, Jacob Andreas.....	38	"	14, 10, 8	6, 4	"
Shwygart, Frederick........	34	"	6, 3, 1½	7, 4	"
Lutz, John George..........	49	"	3	14, 10, 8	Ref.
Meyer, John John..........	25	"			Cath.
Weibel, John Jacob........	36	"	8	10, 6, 3, 1¼	Luth.
Vogel, John (also a carpenter)...................	47	"	6	7, 3	"
Muller, Valentine.........	32	"	6		"
Emmich, Paulus...........	30	"			"
Fuhrer, John..............	40	"	13, 6	8, 1	Cath.
Cunitz, John..............	33	"	15, 5	1	"
Holzer, John (also a hunter).	40	"	3		"

NAME	AGE	WIFE	SONS	DAUS.	CHURCH
Caselman, Christin.........	37	wife	2		Luth.
Hertzog, Casper....	34	"	7, 4		Ref.
Geiger, David..............	50	"	23, 10	5, 4	"
Jacob, Christian............	34	"	8, 5, 2		"
Ade, John.................	36	"	17, 5	15, 5	Luth.
Stauch, John Peter.........	44	"	12, 9, 2	5	Ref.
Mattern, William..........	30	"	4		Luth.
Kopf, Henrich.............	38	"	12	10, 7, 3	Ref.
Kroen, John George........	36	"		2	"
Henckel, John George......	38	"			Cath.
Klaus, Henrich............	36	"		7, 2	
Mattern, John George......	40	"	14, 4, 1	20, 17, 8	Luth.
Otzenberger, John Peter....	40	"		1	Cath.
Keller, John................	28	"	2		"
Heidman, Gerhard.........	20	sing.			Ref.
Becker, Frederick..........	23	"			Luth.
Eckart, Balzar.............	23	wife	2		Cath.
Sternberger, John Jacob....	29	"	10, 7, 4	9	Luth.
Zeiter, John George........	38	"	8	12	"
Ritweil, Frederick..........	32	"	2		"
Ritweil, Jacob..............	22	sing.			"
Peter, John................	38	wife		2	
Misemer, Daniel...........	28	"	3	5, 1½	Luth.
Misemer, Valentine.........	23	"	3, 1		"
Baltz, John Philip..........	18	sing.			"
Keller, Nicol..............	24	wife			Ref.
Roth, John................	24	sing.			Luth.
Werbel, John Wilhelm.....	23	"			"
Crammer, Christian.........	24	"			"
Peters, Henrich............	24	"			Ref.
Tiel, Bernard..............	40	wife	13, 10, 2	18, 11, 6, 4	Ref.
Diestel, Peter Daube.......	24	sing.			
Friel, William.............	50	wife	9	13	Luth.
Buehler, John..............	53	"		20, 14, 1	Ref.
Jordan, Conrad............	21	sing.			
Meurer, John Quirinus......	53	wife	23, 17	26, 24	Luth.
Schneider, Bernard.........	48	"	18, 16	11	"
Schmidt, John William.....	54	"	4, 3	8, 6	"
Meyer, John Joseph........	24	"	1		Ref.
Eberhard, John............	30	"	16, 14, 12	6	Cath.
Bach, John (also gardner)...	38	"	7	13, 11	"
Muller, Henrich.............	48	"	24, 16, 12	18, 9	"
Hartbeck, Matthew.........	30	"			"
Eckstedt, John George......	22				
Langbein, Cristoph.........	25				Luth.
Keller, John Jacob........	24	wife	3		"
Gerby, John Michael.......	29	"	7	3	Ref.
Hust, Jacob...............	52	"	18		"
Beuhman (Beukman?), Michael	24				"
Lang, John.................	49	wife	17, 12, 6	18, 6	
Harnish, John.............	24	"	2		Ref.
Frick, Henrich.............	30	"			Luth.
Bonus, Julius..............	31	"	15, 6, 2		Ref.
Ziegler, Henrich...........	50	"	¾		"
Imberger, Andreas.........	22				Luth.
Hahn, Johann Martin.......	30	wife			Cath.
Martin, Matthew..........	50	"	11, 5	18, 12	"
Klein, Jacob..............	24				Luth.
Oberitter, John Georg......	37	wife	5	10, 2	Cath.
Bush, Christian............	16				Luth.

NAME	AGE	WIFE	SONS	DAUS.	CHURCH
Bush, Philip..............	26	wife	15, 10	8, 3, ½	Luth.
Sprosser, Anton............	23	"			Cath.
Spanheimer, George........	45	"		11, 9, 7, 1	Ref.
Rauch, John Just..........	49	"	8	18	Luth.
Bonden, John..............	34	"		5, 3, 1	
Stoppelbein, Peter..........	24	"	5, 2 m.		Ref.
Lorentz, Peter............	50	"	10	16, 14, 11	Luth.
Scherz, Jacob.............	25	"	5	2	Ref.
Kuehn, Matthew...........	34	"	2		Cath.
Bauer, Christian............	28	"	1		Ref.
Crass, Philip..............	50	"	12	18, 13, 7, 2	Cath.
Lutz (Lut), John Peter......	29	"	11	3, ½	Luth.
Lut, Anton................	28				Cath.
Keyser, Matthew..........	38	wife		12	Ref.
Venus, John Jacob (also a mason)..................	45	"	14, 12, 8, 7	11	Luth.
Lescher, Sebastian.........	40	"	20, 14, 10, 8, 6	15, 12, 6, 4, 1	"
Vreel, John Nicol..........	29·	"		3	Ref.
Stambach, John Jacob......	28	"			"
Weber, John George.......	34	"	1		"
Hepman, Melchior.........	53	"		17, 12, 8	Luth.
Werner, Michael...........	50	"		14	"
Neubauer, Andrew.........	37	"	19	6, 4	"
Fusz, John................	30	"	½	6, 3	Ref.
Bogenman, Jacob..........	30	"	2, 1½		"
Lorentz, John..............	39	"	2	14, 12, 10, 5, 5	"
Seitz, John Dietrich........	36	"	14	10, 3	"
Krems, John...............	29	"	4		Cath.
Wilmar, Ulric..............	53	"	16		Ref.
Spinlar, Caspar............	41	"	11, 3	18, 3	Cath.
Helwig, Henrich...........	27	"	3		Ref.
Krebs, Peter..............	35	"	4, 2		Luth.
Lickel, Daniel..............	24				Ref.
Arm, David................	52	wife	21, 13, 8	17, 6, 2	"
Buco, Jacob................	28	"	5	3, 1	"
Kennel, Samuel............	25	"	1¼		"
Bason, Nicol...............	34	"	6, 4		"
Richard, Peter.............	34	"	13, 1	5, 3	
Thal, Philip................	45	"	20, 3	10, 7, 3	Ref.
Schwegars, John Heinrich..	38	"	6, 1		Luth.
Balmus, Nicol..............	28	"	3	2	"
Herber, John Jacob...... ..	18				"
Lash, Jacob...............	46	wife		23, 18	"
Schreckenberg, John Henrich....................	28	"		3	Cath.
Waldman, Leonhard.......	36	"	5	3, 1½	Luth.
Schombert, John Jacob.....	36	"	3		"
Keyser, John Michel........	46	"	14, 6	11, 3	
Port, Justus...............	30	"		8, 2	Ref.
Eyler, John Conradt........	30				"
Kraut, John George........	28	wife			"
Kieser, John Adam........	29	"			"
Erhardt, John Simon.......	46	"	6, 3	8	"
Helm, John Adam..........	44	"			Cath.
Dunger, John..............	20				"
Fisher, Simon..............	30	wife			"
Casselman, John.....,.....	49	"	10, 3	19, 13, ½	Luth.
Pfadheucher, Marcel.......	52			30, 22	"
Pfadheucher, Hans Henrich	27	wife	10, 3	4	"

NAME	AGE	WIFE	SONS	DAUS.	CHURCH
Riesenbucher, Mattheus....	27	wife	4, 2	7	Luth.
Richter, John Andreas......	46	"	14	17, 7, 3	"
Shaeffer, Andreas (also a carpenter)...............	42	"	13	15, 7	Ref.
Umbach, John George......	35	"		7, 5	"
Depper, Lobonus...........	41	"	16, 1½	12, 4	Cath.
Duerr, Peter (also a carpenter).................	37	"	4	8, 2	Ref.
Rose, John Christoph.......	45	"	16, 12, 9, 7, 3, 1 d.	2	Luth.
Lambert, John.............	65	"	11, 8	13, 9	Cath.
Blaum, Herman............	50	"	6	12	Ref.
Fink, Andreas.............	34	"	9		"
Lutz, John (also a carpenter)	35	"	8, 6, 3	¼	Cath.
Wille, Henrich George.....	36	"	9, 7	2	Luth.
Holtzschuch, John Jacob....	31	"		16, 4	"
Fischbach, John...........	35	"	10, 1	3	"
Wentz, John George........	30	"	4	6	"
Mueller, Peter........	36	"	3	10	"
Gemelk, Michel............	30	"	1		"
Tuebell, Anton.............	40	"	12	9, 4	"
Graeff, Henry..............	44	"	4	12, 6	"
Schaeffer, Henry...........	43	"	20, 17	14	Ref.
Bernard, John George (also a carpenter).............	36	"	5, 1	3	Luth.
Klingelstein, Nicol.........	36	"	7, 3	5, 1	Ref.
Roth, John Peter...........	29	"	3, 1½		Luth.
Brunn, John Tiel...........	35	"		¼	Cath.
Moor, Cleman.............	33	"	6, 2	8, 4	Ref.
Koerner, Wolf.............	30	"	4, 2		Luth.
Wordman, John............	40	"	10, 5	13, ½	Ref.
Wollhand, Engelhard......	26	"			"
Habig, Conrad.............	50	"	24, 21	16	Luth.
Shmidt, Caspar...	58	"	16, 14, 6, 3	27, 24, 10, 7	Cath.
Busch, Caspar (also a hunter)	22	"		2	Luth.
Minglen, Kilian............	36	"	9	11, 7	Ref.
Muntrian, Paul.............	38	"	8, 6, 4		Cath.
Rendel, John Peter.........	43	"		2	Luth.
Oster, Arnd...............	24	"			Cath.
Debald, Francis............	30	"	7, 5, 3		Ref.
Debald, Conrad............	27	"	2	8, 5, 4	"
Rufenacht, Benedict........	46	"	9	13, 11, 6, ¼	"
Daul, John Michael........	22	"			Luth.
Boehm, John Martin........	30	"			"
Riet, John George..........	50	"	20, 18, 16, 14, 7	22, 12, 10	"
Schaefer, Just Henry.......	35	"	9	4	Ref.
Fuhrman, John Michel.....	47	"		13, 7, 4	Luth.
Fuss, Andreas.............	34	"	9, 6	11, 3	Ref.
Kennleiter, John...........	38	"	6, 2	4	Luth.
Heischer, John (also a linen-weaver),.................	30	"	5, ¼	6	"
Ludorf, Conrad............	19				Ref.
Ruehl, John Peter..........	20				Luth.
Kuehn, Conrad............	40	wife	14, 11, 8, 2		Ref.
Boltz, George.............	50	"	13, 7, 4		"
Beck, John Jacob....	50	"	18	20, 13, 10, 8, 6	Luth.
Bergman, Abraham........	46	"	10	19, 16, 14, 7	"
Zwick, Matthew...........	35	"	11, 6, 5	13	"
Moret, Jacob...............	45	"		18, 13, 11	Ref.

NAME	AGE	WIFE	SONS	DAUS.	CHURCH
Bash, Daniel...............	45	wife		18	Ref.
Mutin, Peter...............	30	"	5	20	"
Duester, John..............	34	"	9, 3, ½	6	"
Schnell, Matthew...........	48				Cath.
WHEELWRIGHTS					
Kuntze, Nicol..............	33	wife	8, 7, 4	½	Ref.
Korman, Peter Jacob.......	50	"	20	19	Luth.
Kortner, Peter.............	46	"	11, 8, 6		Ref.
von dem Sabelgaul, John Leonhardt..............	28	"		2	Cath.
Lutz, John Adam...........	22				Luth.
SMITHS					
Weber, John Adolf.........	18				Ref.
Bauer, Elias...............	23				"
Seyfried, John Jacob........	23				Luth.
Herman, Sebastian.........	23				"
Muller, John Ludiger.......	22				Ref.
Kopf, John.................	30				Cath.
Unstat, Valentin...........	22				Luth.
Weber, John Philip.........	18				"
Wolf, John Michel.........	27				"
TAILORS					
Paular, Andreas Jacob......	20				Ref.
Ludwig, John.............	35	wife	10, 1	5	
Frederik, Wendel..........	50	"	8	18, 4, ½	Luth.
Siegler, John Conrad.......	20				Ref.
Wentzel, John Georg.......	20				Luth.
Petri, Henry...............	20				Ref.
Ulrich, Cristof.............	30	wife	2	7, 3	Luth.
——, Daniel................	24				Ref.
Fink, John Godfried........	44		18, 10		Luth.
Liebhan, John..............	36		12		Cath.
Stoll, John.................	16				"
Aman, John................	27	wife			Ref.
Kleus, John................	24	"		½	"
Shaefer, Georg.............	18				"
Deibolt, John Georg	20				"
Schretz, Michael...........	18				Cath.
Kleus, Carl................	16				Ref.
Muschel, Jacob.............	25	wife	½		Luth.
Barrabam, John Wolf.......	34	"		4, 2	Ref.
LINEN WEAVERS					
Jacky, Ulrich..............	31				Ref.
Eck, Velentin..............	50	wife	16, 10, 7	12, 5	Cath.
Shaar, Daniel..............	24				Ref.
Cauer, Jacob Mitter........	40	wife	5, 3	1	Luth.
Becke, Ephraim.....	32	"	4, 3		"
Haber, Barthel.............	29	"	¾	11, 6, 4	"
Frauch, Georg.............	30	"	5, 2		Ref.
Bastian, Andreas...........	21				Cath.
Ludolph, John.............	31	wife	5, 3	7, ½	Ref.
WOOLEN WEAVERS					
Dufin, Peter...............	53				Ref.
Hero, Henrich.............	33	wife	8	5	"
Schwartz, Christian........	36				"

NAME	AGE	WIFE	SONS	DAUS.	CHURCH
Jung, Abraham (a shoe-maker).................	18				Ref.
Kless, Henry (a shoemaker).	37	wife	6, 1	10, 8, 4	Luth.
Kauffer, Daniel (also a shoe-maker).................	27				"
BAKERS					
Martin, Thomas............	24				Luth.
Kling, John Conrad.........	22				"
Sigmund, John Michel......	27	wife	1		Ref.
Kornman, John Peter.......	37	"	5	1	"
Marx, Matthew............	23				Cath.
Schmotzer, John Jacob......	33	wife	4	12	Luth.
Windeberger, John Jacob..	35	"	12, 3	10, 5	"
Weber, John Caspar........	20				Ref.
Hartwig, Caspar...........	38	wife	5, 4	7	"
Muller, John Jacob.........	30	"	1	1	"
MASONS AND STONE CUTTERS					
Kremmeln, Salomon........	23				Ref.
Meister, Jacob.............	24				"
Philip, George Thomas.....	40	wife			Luth.
Hernichel, Henrich.........	46	"	5	9, 2	Ref.
Vogelsperger, Joachim.....	30				Cath.
Winhofer, John Georg......	28				"
Stephen, John.............	36	wife	2		"
Bishop, Ludwig...........	19				Luth.
Garter, John (Englishman)..	40				Ref.
CARPENTERS					
Frey, Henrich.............	27	wife		½	Ref.
John, Cristoph.............	33				Luth.
Flegler, Zacharra...........	36	wife	8, 4	1	"
Semter, John.............	38	"	2	.	Ref.
Dalem, Lambert...........	27	"		5	Cath.
Codd, John................	26				Luth.
Riesenburn, Jacob..........	37				Cath.
Wambach, Nicol...........	36	wife	12, 8, 5, 2		"
Mueller, John Nicol........	22				"
Mueller, Jacob.............	37	wife	14, 10, 4	6, 3	"
Fuehrer, John Jacob........	26				"
Hartung, Caspar...........	25				Luth.
Schueler, Franciscus.......	42				Cath.
Dietz, John Peter...........	26				"
BUTCHERS					
Jung, John.................	28	wife			Ref.
Trep, John Jacob...........	28	"			"
Clanenberg, Conrad........	38	"		1	Luth.
MILLERS					
Selner, John Adam.........	51	wife		5, 2	Luth.
Schuch, John Peter.........	32	"		12, 10	Cath.
Stein, John................	44	"			"
Muller, John..............	24				Luth.
COOPERS AND BREWERS					
Baehr, Tobias.............	45	wife	11, 9, 6, 3	14	Ref.
Matthew, John.............	37	"	8, 5	11	Cath.
Hartman, John Georg......	28	"	1		Luth.

NAME	AGE	WIFE	SONS	DAUS.	CHURCH
Milbert, John Martin.......	40	wife	13	11, 2	Luth.
Lutz, Cristoph.............	36				Ref.
Bruder, Valentin...........	25	wife			"
Mehder, John Henry........	28				"
JOINERS					
Tibold, Isaac..............	48	wife			Ref.
Schultheis, John...........	26	"	½	2	Luth.
Ellenberger, George........	45	"	15		Ref.
Crukot, Arnold.............	42	"	2	8	"
Dinant, Peter.............	39	"	11, 9, 7, 5	3	"
TURNERS					
Mueckel, Ulrich...........	36	wife	3, 1		Ref.
Teske, Jacob..............	50	"	20, 16		Luth.
Hofman, Gabriel...........	40				Ref.
Hatteman, Ulrich..........	40	wife	10, 4	9, 5, 2	Mennon.
SADDLER					
Rudolf, John..............	20				Ref.
LABOURERS					
Wagner, Andreas..........	37	wife	6, 3		Cath.
Helm, Peter..............	30	"	15,11,9,6, 4, ¼	7	Ref.
SILVERSMITHS					
Reinhold, John Georg......	27				Luth.
Schmiedel, Siegmund.......	24				Ref.
TANNERS					
Jung, Jacob...............	25				Ref.
Jacob, John (apothecary)....	21				Luth.
Beck, John (merchant's apprentice)..............	22				"
WIDOWS					
Bieco, Mary Lucas.........	52		25, 14	18, 11, 8	Ref.
Rockeln, Elizabeth.........	77				Luth.
Lichtnerin, Margaret.......	50				Ref.
Lichtnerin, Anna Maria.....	30		2		
Dinkelin, Appolonia........	80				Luth.
Plazerin, Sarah............	36		2	10	"
Schultheis, Esther Susanna.	46		20, 9	11, 6, 4	"
Jungin, Elizabeth..........	49		24, 12	19, 16	Luth.
Mutten, Anna Maria..	50				Ref.
Bingerin, Elizabeth........	24			2	"
Emmoch, Anna Eve........	44		21, 18		"
Kleinsin, Gertrud..........	48		14	11, 8	"
Mushelin, Anne Marg......	50		16		"
Steigerin, Cristina.........	60				"
Schaker, Susanne..........	70				"
Krebsin, Salome...........	50				"
UNMARRIED WOMEN					
Weiss, Mary..............	34				Ref.
Weiss, Magdalena.........	30				"
Barrabam, Anna Clara......	23				"
Dresin, Gerdrut...........	30				Cath.
Weritzen, Anne Catherine..	27				"
Kellerin, Barbara..........	21				Ref.
Schutmegenn, Charlotta....	26				Cath.

NAME	AGE	WIFE	SONS	DAUS.	CHURCH
Kiesenn, Anne Catherine...	18				Cath.
Woberin, Eva..............	22				Ref.
Barba, Anna...............	18				Cath.
Klessin, Maria............	24				Luth.
Melkin, Anna Margaretha..	22				"
Guthman, Maria Barbara...	22				Cath.
Reichardin, Anna Barba....	20				"
Welkin, Maria.............	30				Ref.
Koernerin, Maria..........	24				"
Obermullerin, Mary Catherine...................	30				"
Hartwegin, Anne Elizabeth.	22				Luth.
Margareth, Elizabeth......	20				
Wunderlich, Christina......	21				Cath,
Bessenn, Dorethea.........	25				Luth.

THE WHOLE SUM:

```
Men.............................. 311
Women ........................... 263
Sons ............................ 323
Daughters........................ 296
                                 ─────
                                 1193
```

(ENDORSED)

A second list of 1193 Palatines lately arrived from Germany, distinguishing their Professions, Ages, etc.

LISTS OF GERMANS FROM THE PALATINATE WHO CAME TO ENGLAND IN 1709.

The following lists are copied from the original documents preserved in the British Museum Library, London, England, and should be of the greatest genealogical interest to those families in the States of New York, New Jersey, Pennsylvania and elsewhere, which claim descent from the so-called Palatine settlers. These lists have never before been printed to the knowledge of the Editor, and it should be noted that the word "son" or "sons" and "dau." or "daus." followed by figures denote that the heads of the family had as many sons or daughters, as there are figures, and that these sons and daughters were of the respective ages denoted by the figures. The word "wife" indicates that the head of the family was married and that the wife was living. The abbreviations "Ref.," "Luth.," "Bap." and "Cath.," mean that the family belonged to the Reformed, Lutheran, Baptist or Catholic Churches.

BOARD OF TRADE MISCELLANEOUS. VOL. 2. NO. D 68.

PUBLIC RECORD OFFICE, LONDON.

List of the poor Palatines that are arrived in St. Cathrin's, the 2nd of June, 1709.

THIRD ARRIVALS.

NAME	AGE	WIFE	SONS	DAUS.	CHURCH
HUSBANDMEN & VINEDRESSERS					
Kuehlman, John..........	50	wife		20, 12, 9, 7, 2	Ref.
Reckhart, Justus..........	53	"			Luth.
Weber, Martin.............	34	"		3, ¾	
Glass, Valentine..........	25	"			Cath.
Molendueck, Herman......	50	"		19, 12	Ref.
Stuetz, Johan.............	35	"	13, 6	11, 3	Cath.
Luetz, John George........	30	"		2	Ref.
Lutz, Peter...............	40	"	7, 2	10	"
Hildebrand, Johan........	50	"	11	15	Luth.
Heumacher, John Jacob.....	30	"	3, 2		Cath.
Schweitzer, Michael.......	28	"	2, ½		Luth.
Schneider. Johan George....	38	"	11	6	"
Fechter, Martin...........	40	"	6	18, 15, 10, 3, 1½	"
Hartman, Conrad.........	45	"		4	"
Mohr, Christoph...........	40	"			"
Schiefer, Johan...........	42	"	9, 5, 3	1½	"
Beydelman, Johan Michel..	40	"	7, 5	9	
Lemp, Conrad.............	36	"	7	3	Ref.
Igelsbach, Wendal.........	45	"	4, 2	6, ½	"
Wegman, Mattheus........	35	"	11, 9, ½	13, 7, 6, 3	"
Graf, Philip Leonhardt.....	48	"	15	18, 12, 9, 4	"
Lehrers, Johan Philip.......	30	"		13	"
Thomas, Matheus.........	42	"	4	11, 8, ¼	"

NAME	AGE	WIFE	SONS	DAUS.	CHURCH
Meyer, Henrich............	43	wife	11	13	Luth.
Brandlin, Caspar...........	42	"	4	½	Cath.
Schlosser, John.............	54	"		14, 8	"
Anweiler, John.............	27	"	1		"
Stieb, John Reinhard.......	48	"	12, 9	23, 18	Luth.
Stieb, John Peter..........	45	"	5, 3	¾	"
Helfer, Cristop.............	40	"	8, 2	6	"
Muller, George Philip......	36	"	11, 6	8, 5, 1	"
Lobwasser, Anton..........	41	"	7		Cath.
Tag, Francis Hendrich....	47	"	9	11	Luth.
Meyer, Jacob..............	32	"	2		"
Schnidt, John Jacob........	25	"	¾		"
Nakhan, William...........	38	"		5, ½	Ref.
Bunderskeil, Andreas.......	40	"	14, 7	15, 7	Cath.
Herman, Schweikhart......	40	"	19, 6	4	"
——, Matheus.............	23	"	1		"
Neumeyer, John August....	35	"	3	12, 8, 6	"
Quint, Anton..............	36	"	4, 3	3	"
Weber, Philip.............	60	"	20		"
Hunold, Seyfart...........	38	"	16, 14, 12, 3, ½	9, 5	Luth.
Craemer, Philip............	35	"			Cath.
Thomas, Francis...........	28	"	2		"
Gross, William.............	24	"	4	1½	Ref.
Ritz, John.................	40	"	10	6, 1½	Cath.
Weimar, Simon............	40	"	10, 8	5	Luth.
Conrads, Conrad...........	36	"		10, 1	Cath.
Charton, Hendrick.........	32	"		19, 6, 4, 1½	"
Wilmart, John Martin......	35	"	10, 5	13, 8, 5	"
Kolbe, Francis.............	36	"	20, 14, 10, 7	15	"
Beckart, Conrad...........	30	"	10, 1½	4	"
Fink, John Adam...........	24(?)	"	16(?)	1	"
Kast, John George.........	30	"	8	6, 4, 2	Luth.
Westhofer, Johan Jacob.....	30	"	2		Ref.
Paul, John Daniel.........	59	"		36, 33, 30, 20	"
Paul, John, Clother........	46	"	18, 7	9, 4	Luth.
Wrikedy, Philip............	30	"	7	1	Cath.
Hayn, John................	40	"	16	12, 7, 1½	"
Musier, John Jacob.........	54	"	24, 12, 9, 3	21, 18	Ref.
Schwing, John.............	23	"			"
Sex, Philip.................	53	"	20, 5	16, 13, 1½	Luth.
Weber, Henrik.............	32	"	13, 10, 1	7	Ref.
Hammerleim, John Jacob...	45	"	13	11, 7, 2	"
Egelman, John Adam......	37	"	2	8, 6	Luth.
Cays, John Brill (a shoe-maker	45	"	18, 17	15, 11	Ref.
Braun, John Debauld.......	58	"	¼		"
Gedel, John Peter..........	27	"	¾		"
Dorn, Lazarus.............	48	"	14, 7	10, 9, 6, 1½, ¼	"
Schaefer, John Andreas.....	42	"	11, 7, 1	12, 4, 4	Luth.
Zwinger, George Peter......	40	"	21, 2		Cath.
Seip, John Peter............	27	"		2	Ref.
Muench, Christoph.........	26	"	1		Luth.
Hillig, Andreas............	26	"	2		"
Hop, Christian.............	35	"			"
Straub, John...............	26	"		¼	"
Reisenberger, Lorentz......	46	"	2	9, 6	Ref.
Brummer, Johan....... ...	40	"	7, 1		Cath.
Knaub, Johan Christoph	30	"	2	1	Ref.

NAME	AGE	WIFE	SONS	DAUS.	CHURCH
Rautebusch, Johan.........	30	wife		3	Luth.
Geschwind, Johan..........	35	"	7	5, 3, 1	Cath.
Gusman, Peter.............	40	"	8, 7, 1		"
Kraut, John Peter..........	38	"	1	10, 7, 4	Ref.
Mey, Christoph............	35	"		3	"
Hoechst, Burckard.........	27	"	5, ¼		Luth.
Ortminger, Nicol...........	34	"	7, 5	3, 1	Cath.
Emmerich, Peter...........	36	"		5	Ref.
Eyler, Johann..............	50	"	15, 3, 3 m.	12, 10, 8, 4	"
von der Muehler, Philip....	51	"	19, 1½	22, 17, 14, 13, 11, 7	"
Weber, Henry.............	52	"	16, 8, 6	2, ½	"
Neuman, Ludwig...........	37	"	12, 9, 6	9, 6	"
Appel, Christian...........	37	"		6, 3	Cath.
Reinhard, Henry...........	28	"	2		Luth.
Baehr, Frederick...........	29	"	4, 2		Cath.
Lentz, Henry..............	40	"	11, 9, 2		"
Schaeffer, Gerhard.........	30	"	6, 3, 1		"
Rhode, Johan Juste.........	28	"	3, 1	5	Ref.
Rup, Johan................	52	"		23, 20	Luth.
Dolmetsch, Johan..........	30	"	12, 9, 6	2, ½	"
Hecht, Caspar.............	50	"	24, 11, 9, 7, 2	27, 18	"
Beker, Michel.............	32	"	6	4	Ref.
Flor, Johan...............	46	"	23	25	"
Mentz, Anton.............	28	"	8	6	Cath.
Henrich, Johan James......	23	"			Luth.
Falck, Arnold.............	32	"	6, 2		Cath.
Muster, Lambert..........	50	"	25	15	"
Strauch, Johan............	30	"	2		Luth.
Hill, John William.........	40	"	1	5, 4	Ref.
Hill, Johan.	90				"
Nuentzeberger, Dieterich...	51	wife	17, 13, 10, 8, 4	19, 15	Cath.
Madler, Michel............	38	"	11, 7, 4	18	Luth.
Streit, Ludwig.............	42	"	8, 6	5, 3, ½	Cath.
Dungel, Matthey..........	33				"
Derding, Conrad...........	30				Luth.
Gross, Frederick..........	36	wife	3	1	"
Eckhard, Balzar...........	60	"		21, 18	Cath.
Kuml, Johan Peter........	40	"	20, 16, 12, 10, 5	18	"
Schenkelberger, Johan Jacob	36	"	3	21,18,16,1	"
Bungart, Jacob.............	51	"	15		"
Bohne, Francis.............	39	"	10, 9	5	"
Bungart, Matthew..........	24	"		4, 1	"
Bungart, William..........	26	"	4, 2		"
Cleman, Bastian...........	44	"	21, 16, 7	10, 8	Ref.
Cleman, Valentine.........	20	"	1½		"
Stock, Johan Henrich.......	33	"			Luth.
Eckard, Johan Jacob.......	24	"			Ref.
Buchebuerger, Johan Nicol.	53	"	11, 9, 5, ¾	9	Luth.
Wagner, Wendel...........	36	"	11, 4	9, 1 m.	"
Bishhoff, George Henrich...	28	"		6, 2	"
Plsch, Benedict	55	"	3	6, 2	Cath.
Wagner, Ernst Ludwig.....	40	"	16, 13, 10, 6, 3	10	Luth.
Shmith, Philip.............	42	"	13, 8	11, ¾	Ref.
Weigel, Valentine..........	43	"	11, 4	7, 6	Cath.
Hofferling, Henrich........	54	"	24	22, 21, 18	"
Engel, Johan Rupert.......	42	"	21, 17, 14	12	"

NAME	AGE	WIFE	SONS	DAUS.	CHURCH
Mey, Johan Peter..........	38	wife		7, 5	Cath.
Johan, Henry...............	36	"	11, 9	5, 3	"
Reisdorf, Johan............	34	"	1	4	"
Creylach, Urban...........	50	"		18	Luth.
Apfel, Johan Jacob.........	21				Cath.
Petri, Nicol...............	38	wife	7	10, 1½	Luth.
Wagner, Valentine.........	48	"	7	13, 10	Cath.
Zentgraf, Johan Hendrich...	37	"	8, 2 m.	10, 6	Luth.
Simon, Philip..............	25	"			Ref.
Engel, Martin..............	36	"	13, 10, 2	5	Cath.
Schmif, Nicol..............	45	"	11, 6	3	"
Vogt, Daniel...............	46	"	7, 2	1	"
Tresanus, Johan............	45	"	20, 4	22, 16	"
Hermes, Johan.............	27	"		2	"
Klein, Johan Michael.......	40	"	11, 9, 7, 5	4	"
Puppelritter, Christian......	43	"	5	20, 10, 12	"
Vogt, Johan................	63	"	15, 8	10	Ref.
Zweller, Philip.............	44	"	12, 5	15	Cath.
Leinweber, Johan..........	36	"	14	9	Ref.
Boller, Philip.............	36	"	11, 9, 7	4, 2½	"
Gerhard, Valentine.........	38	"		13, 11, 6, 4, 1	"
Penner, Henry.............	30	"	6, 4	¼	"
Erbs, Johan Henry.........	25	"	6, 4, ¼		"
Molsberger, Philip.........	30	"		4	"
Close, Peter...............	50	"	20, 11, 8	24, 13	"
Ramp, Nicol...............	37	"	13, 5	10, 2	
Dales, William.............	36	"	4, 1	6	Ref.
Schneider, Conrad..........	33	"		8, 5	"
Paul, Gerhard.............	52	"	24, 11	27, 18, 10, 8, 6	"
Abel, Michael..............	29	"	½	3	Cath.
Proebstel, George..........	40	"	7	11	"
Ruhl, John Caspar (also a linen weaver)............	25	"			Luth.
Freisen, John Riccas.......	27	"	2	3, ¼	Cath.
Hill, Balzar (also a carpenter)...................	45	"	16, 14, 10	18, 7	"
Merstallen, Henry..........	41	"	10, 5, 1	7, 6	Luth.
Rufel, John Nicol	49	"	17, 12, 5	21, 19, 7	"
Meyer, Nicol...............	33	"		10, 5, ½	Ref.
Fohrer, John (also a tanner).	60	"	20, 18		Cath.
Stork, John Henry..........	45	"	28, 18, 8, 6	12	Luth.
Fohrer, John...............	25	"		2	Cath.
Beisser, John..............	50	"	30, 20	18, 11	Ref.
Koerner, John Nicol........	50	"	6, 3	9, 4	"
Mandersel, John Peter......	24	"			Cath.
Seiffart, John..............	43	"	13	10, 8, 2	Luth.
Schaeffer, Matthew........	40	"	8		Ref.
Kraus, John George........	62				"
Wolf, John George........	37	wife	7, 2	10, 4	Luth.
Niedermeyer, Andrew......	43	"	6	11, 9, 5	Cath.
Benter, John Just..........	23	"	2		Luth.
Schmidt, Michel...........	50	"	18, 7	20, 14, 4	"
Diggart, Andreas..........	30	"	5		Ref.
Bode, John George........	20	"			"
Wentzel, Lorentz..........	29	"		10, 8, 6, 4, 1	Luth.
Schaefer, John Peter.......	34	"			"
Walter, Adam..............	50	"	15, 12, 4	6	Cath.
Ruhl, Jacob................	42	"	22, 12	17, 16, 10	"
Michel, Otto Henry........	30	"	1		"

NAME	AGE	WIFE	SONS	DAUS.	CHURCH
Schuch, Nicholas..........	24	wife		4, 1 ½	Ref.
Koenig, Justis.............	36	"	7	12	"
Dorninger, Caspar.........	36	"	4	10	"
Spengeler, Frederick......	53	"	20, 11		"
Strassberger, Frederick....	26	"	3		"
Emmel, John..............	36	"		4	
Braun, Sebastian..........	48	"	10	12, 5	Ref.
Spengler, Frantz..........	30	"			"
Lutz, Peter...............	27	"	2	8, 5	"
Keselbach, John...........	40	"	12	1, 5	Cath.
Heil, Matthew.............	30	"			Ref.
Christshiles, William.......	35	"		10, 8, 5, 2	Cath.
Christshiles, Dominic,......	76	"	18		"
Schmaleberger, Cill........	26	"	2		"
Mehs, Paul...............	24	"			"
Wehr, Christian...........	54	"		22	Ref.
Bauer, Thomas............	40	"	14, 12, 10, 8, 7	19, 16,13, 9	Cath.
Martin, Nicol.............	51	"	21		Ref.
Debald, Martin...........	30	"	10	8, 2	"
Schum, John George........	35	"			Luth.
Schrer, Ulrich............	30	"	10, 8		Ref.
Schmidt, Andrew..........	47	wife	4	20,14,11,7	Luth.
Bubeheiser, John Adam....	57	"	20, 15, 13, 12, 4	21, 19, 15, 12,8	Ref.
Big, John.................	36	"	16, 8		Luth.
Titschke, John.............	30	"	4	1	Ref.
Braun, John..............	39	"	12, 9, 4, 1	7, 5, 3	Luth.
Graehl, Lorentz...........	27	"	1		"
Mick, John...............	23	"			Ref.
Mick, Frederick...........	65	"	23, 18	28, 26	Cath.
Mick, Henry..............	35	"	9, 5	12, 7	Ref.
Spiess, Werner............	50	"	11, 5	14, 9	"
Schmidt, Daniel...........	33	"	2	4	"
Lesch, Balzar.............	38	"	14, 8, 2	9	Luth.
Walter, John Jacob........	41	"	7	10	Ref.
Weitz, John...............	35	"	6, 1	8	Luth.
Mathes, Henry............	42	"	8, 6, 1	13, 10, 6	Ref.
Bredhauer, Israel..........	43	"	6, 1	9, 3	Luth.
Zeg, John................	42	"	1, 6, ½		Cath.
Sprehd, Ignatius...........	28	"	3		"
Wagner, John.............	46	"	6, 2		"
Kuhn, Henry.............	53	"	8	10	Luth.
Koehler, John Simon.......	42	"	6	2, 2 m.	Ref.
Kuenstler, Henry..........	36	"	5	2	"
Eybach, Reinhard..........	50	"	20, 16	25	"
Maul, Johan Henry........	48	"	8	13,11,4, ½	"
Haas, Nicol...............	44	"	7, 4, 1	10	Luth.
Merich, George...........	53	"	20, 15, 5		"
Muuer, Caspar............	42	"	12, 10		Cath.
Walter, Philip.......	21	"	6, 3, 1		Ref.
Tiel, Johann..............	22	"			Cath.
Goerher, Sebastian.........	23	"	1		Ref.
Mauer, John Jacob........	22	"			Cath.
Geyer, Johan David........	34	"	4	12, 9, 2	Luth.
Hargart, Johan Nicol.......	30	"	14, ½	8	"
Reck, Jacob..............	50	"	20	16, 14	Cath.
Lipper, Johan Jacob........	30	"	13, 8	1	"
Rentel, Johan Nicol.......	46	"	16, 12	5	Luth.
Brauch, Johan Valentine....	34	"	6, 5		"
Schmidt, Johan............	34	"	1	9	Ref.

NAME	AGE	WIFE	SONS	DAUS.	CHURCH
Schmidt, Caspar..........	50	wife	18, 13, 11	20	Ref.
Lieborn, Ludwig...........	30	"		2	Luth.
Nacheigall, Johan Conrad...	26	"	2	5	"
Knut, Nicol...............	32	"	9		Cath.
Schleyer, Johan...........	40	"		8, 4, ½	"
Feldnacht, Johan..........	37	"	3, ½		"
Land, Philip..............	24	"			"
Lauber, Johan.............	30	"		9, 6, 3	"
Becker, Hendrick..........	53	"	20, 19, 15, 11	22, 18, 16, 13	"
Guth, Johan...............	36	"	10, 6	11	"
Lorentz, Michel...........	48	"	20, 18	15	"
Sarburger, Wenceslag......	43	wife	9, 7	13, 2	Ref.
Schnell, Matthew..........	43	"	17,13,10,5	7	Luth.
Sarburger, August........	36	"	2	5	Ref.
Sarburger, Johan..........	25	"		3, 1	"
Herbener, Henrich........	40	"	12	6, 3	Luth.
Hack, Conrad.............	80	"	16, 9		Ref.
Klein, Jacob.............	48	"	20		Luth.
Tielman, Johan...........	30	"			Cath.
Geney, Jacob.............	50	"	22, 20	18, 16, 14, 11, 7	"
Heins, Johan Valentine....	33	"		10, 3	Luth.
Ebeling, Johan............	35	"	14, 10	8, 1	Cath.
Winter, Henry............	40	"	13, 6	14, 11	"
Leonhard, Johan Peter.....	24	"		½	"
Fuhrman, Johan Mathew...	32	"			Luth.
Schneider, Johan..........	30	"	7		"
Edian, Sebastian..........	32	"		2	"
Keller, Jacob..............	35	"	12,10,8,5	5, 2	Ref.
Ebrecht, John.............	40	"		5. 2	"
Seyfars, Johan Valentine....	44	"	17		"
Wickel, Johan.............	38	"			"
Zink, Rudolf..............	44	"	22, 17, 14	19	"
Hess, Jeremy.............	34	"	7, 5	2	Luth.
Kossing, Anthony..........	30	"			"
Rohn, Johan..............	45	"	20, 18, 16, 12, 8	14, 5, 2	"
Altvater, Johan Valentine...	24	"			Ref.
Weiler, Johan.............	32	"			"
Heyn, Paul...............	39	"	8, 3	11	Luth.
Kurtz, Johan.............	41	"	8	13	Cath.
Pliss, John.	35	"	8, 3	11	Luth.
Boef, Johan..............	41	"	6, 2	4	Cath.
Petisht, Henry............	50	"	14, 9, 12	6, 1	"
Petisht, Johan Dietrich.....	36	"		4	"
Kaul, Francis.............	36	"		2	Luth.
Hartman, Conrad..........	30	"	7	4, ½	Cath.
Bloss, Conrad.............	33	"	8, 6, 2	2 m.	Luth.
Heck, Bastian.............	40	"	6	8, 4	"
Graef, Johan..............	27	"			"
Mehser, Conrad...........	54	"			"
Heinemann, Johan Henrich.	28	"	5	7, 1	Cath.
Kirshner, Philip...........	28	"	5, 2	2	Luth.
Schneider, John...........	29	"	2 m.		"
Beckman, Michel..........	26	"	1	7	Cath.
Boef, William.............	70	"			"
Kraft, Valentin...........	40	wife	6, 4	16, 9, 2	Luth.
Meyer, Johan.............	29	"	7, 3	4	"
Leyser, Christoph..........	56	"	24, 14, 11	20	"
Stiebel, Johann............	36	"	6, 1 m.	8, 4, 2	"

NAME	AGE	WIFE	SONS	DAUS.	CHURCH
Reichard, Caspar..........	24	wife	3, 1		Cath.
Mathes, Johan..............	33	"	15, 10	12	"
Sharnigk, Andrew..........	26	"	4	2	
Klitten, George............	27	"	2		Cath.
Specht, Johan.............	31	"	5	4, ½	"
Stick, Horman.............	40	"	14	8	"
Qurlea, Francis............	50	"	8, 4, 3		"
Klein, Johan William.......	42	"	18	24, 20	"
Mehrman, Johan Just.......	30	"			"
Jung, Johan................	32	"	9	1	"
Freund, Johan..............	46	"	26, 24	19, 17, 14	Ref.
Holtzlaender, Albert........	40	"	5, ¼	14, 9, 4	Cath.
Grosman, Johan............	26	"	2	8, 6	"
Mank, Jacob....	39	"		17, 9, 3	Ref.
Becker, Paulus.............	42	"	14	14, 12	
Falkenburg, Valentin.......	38	"	7, 2		Ref.
Valpert, Jacob.............	40	"	8, 4	10	"
Boher, Andrew.............	40	"			"
Ziegler, Nicol..............	47	"	7	23, 15, 9	"
Petit, Johan Jacob.........	50				"
Busch, Herman.............	54		4	24	Luth.
Schloemer, Mattheas.......	38	wife	¼	8, 3	Ref.
Flor, Johan................	36	"	8, 4	9	Cath.
Laurentz, Nicol............	40	"	15, 11, 5	8	Ref.
Boehm, Frantz.............	44	"	12, 7, 3	20, 18, 5	"
Ludwig, Johan............ .	54	"	20, 25	12, 10	"
Martin, Adam..............	36	"	3	7, 5	"
Boerwg, Michael...........	30	"	½		"
Holles, Henry..............	25	"			"
Tulges, Conrad.............	36	"	8, 4	6, ½	Cath.
Teiss, Peter...............	25	"			Ref.
Wann. Francis.............	30	"	3	5	"
Hess, Friedrich............	42	"	2	11, 7	"
Glass, William.............	36	"	8, 5	3, ¼	Cath.
Otto, Johan................	24	"			Ref.
Weiss, Johan...............	26	"	3	2	"
Feller, Johan..............	45	"	4, 2	12, 9	"
Bergman, Johan Just......:.	32	"	4	8	Cath.
Berger, Veit...............	36	"	3	4	"
Hep (Hess?) Johan Jacob...	28	"		6, 4	Luth.
Braun Andrew.............	26	"	3, 1½	5	Cath.
Villonger, Johan...........	30	"			Ref.
Schautz (Schantz), Johan....	63	"	7	20	"
Meyer, Thomas............	44	"	1	10	"
Schaefert Philip...........	36	"	10	2	Cath.
Knecht, Michael..........	50	"		21, 18, 15, 12	"
Becker, Anton.............	30	"	5	7	"
Schmidt, Nicol......	30	"	2	4, 6 w.	"
Wiennegar, Ulrich.........	41	"	7	11, 14	"
Huber, Jacob..............	30	"	13	10, 7	Luth.
Mohr, Jonas...............	38	"	10		"
Weinmann, Andreas.......	30	"	2	10, 6	"
Wipf, Johan Jacob.........	27	"	½		"
Altheimer, Johan Georg....	40	"	13. 10, 8, 6, 4	11	"
Glaser Georg..............	47	"	5	9	"
Naser, Johan Michael.......	48	"	20, 12	18, 16	"
Medke, Daniel.............	41	"	15	14, 13, 3	"
Steinhauer, Christian.......	46	"	½	25, 22, 19, 16, 4	Cath.

NAME	AGE	WIFE	SONS	DAUS.	CHURCH
Nilius, Jonan..............	34	wife	12, 13	12, 6, ¼	Cath,
Schweitzer, Cristoph.......	23				Luth.
Hill, Johan.................	24				Cath.
Wezel, George.............	14				"
Wezel, John..............	12				"
Eshenbrender, Wolf........	40				"
Ebelman, Jacob............	36				Ref.
Meyer, Johan.............	25				Luth.
Zeber, Joseph.............	30				Cath.
von Rhein, Christian.......	23				Luth.
Burge, Arnold.....	24				Ref.
Paul, Johan	22				"
Gersner, Balzar............	28				Luth.
Muench, Peter.............	24				"
Johan, Johan Michel.......	18				
Meyfart, Jacob.............	12				Ref.
Hop, Michel..............	26				Luth.
Kuhn, Peter..............	24				Ref.
Reichard, Henry...........	25				"
Dungel, Matthew..........	33				Cath.
Belz, Leonhard............	20				"
Koch, Martin..............	28				Luth.
Derding, Conrad...........	30				"
Jaeger, Peter.............	23				Cath.
Traut, Johan..............	20				"
Schreiner, Martin..........	20				
Rup, Georg...............	18				Ref.
Gross, Joachim............	25				Luth.
Claude, Francis...........	22				Ref.
Hoffman, Matthew.........	20				Cath.
Simon, Nicol..............	14				Ref.
Tiefenthaler, George.......	18				Luth.
Kesler, Johan Peter........	21				
Ternbach, Justus..........	18				Ref.
Wolfskeil, Georg..........	28				Luth.
Haub, Christoph..........	20				"
Henninger, Johan Adam....	24				"
Fritzin, Johan.............	36				
Gam, Jacob...............	24				Ref.
Kohl, Johan..............	24				"
Handwerker, Daniel.......	28				"
Handwerker, Peter........	24				
Zimmerman, Caspar.......	28				Luth.
Nick, Johan Jacob.........	15				"
Herman, Conrad...........	23				Ref.
Leperl, Matthew...........	24				"
Wolf, Johan..............	28				Luth.
Ulrich, Johan.............	25				Ref.
Lauer, Matthew...........	23				Luth.
Grien, Friedrick...........	22				Ref.
Hesper, Simon.............	30				Luth.
Hessel, William...........	22				Ref.
Werner, Henry.............	24				
Koch, Johan..............	22				Luth.
Volker, Henry.............	32				"
Rosenthal, Johan..........	30				"
Heins, Adam..............	22				"
Loss, Jacob...............	25				
Schmid, Bernhard.. :......	27				Cath.
Wentz, Balzar.............	24				Luth.
Clos, Peter...............	28				Cath.

LISTS OF GERMANS FROM THE PALATINATE WHO CAME TO ENGLAND IN 1709.

The following lists are copied from the original documents preserved in the British Museum Library, London, England, and should be of the greatest genealogical interest to those families in the States of New York, New Jersey, Pennsylvania and elsewhere, which claim descent from the so-called Palatine settlers. These lists have never before been printed to the knowledge of the Editor, and it should be noted that the word "son" or "sons" and "dau." or "daus." followed by figures denote that the heads of the family had as many sons or daughters, as there are figures, and that these sons and daughters were of the respective ages denoted by the figures. The word "wife" indicates that the head of the family was married and that the wife was living. The abbreviations "Ref.," "Luth.," "Bap." and "Cath.," mean that the family belonged to the Reformed, Lutheran, Baptist or Catholic Churches.

BOARD OF TRADE MISCELLANEOUS. VOL. 2. No. D 68.

PUBLIC RECORD OFFICE, LONDON.

List of the poor Palatines that are arrived in St. Cathrin's, the 2nd of June, 1709.

THIRD ARRIVALS—*Continued.*

NAME	AGE	WIFE	SONS	DAUS.	CHURCH
HUSBANDMEN & VINEDRESSERS					
Kuth, Peter...............	26				Ref.
Sturteweg, Caspar..........	24				"
Schaffer, Lorentz..........	28				"
Homberg, Christian........	18				"
Drummer, Gerard..........	24				"
Becker, Peter.............	28				"
Klein, Ludwig.............	18				"
Bell, Johan Engel..........	27				"
Flor, Peter................	25				Cath.
Schreiber, Albert..........	26				Ref.
Wolf, Peter...............	28				"
Thurdoerf, Friederich......	24				"
Rosbach, Peter.............	28				"
Eslich, Paul...............	21				"
Jung, Adam...............	17				"
Jung, Johan...............	18				"
Knoehl, Herman..........	24				Cath.
Neuss, Andrew............	27				"
Schmids, Christian.........	22				Ref.
Burder, Johan.............	16				"
Noll, Daniell..............	22				"
Middler, William..........	12				"
Eyfel, Helkert............	13				"
Huhn, Matthew............	20				"
Rabenegger, Nicol.........	20				Cath.

NAME	AGE	WIFE	SONS	DAUS.	CHURCH
Scherer, Ebald.............	20				Ref.
Loucks, Philip.............	28				"
SCHOOLMASTERS					
Zinger, Nicol..............	40	wife	12, 6	9, 3	Ref.
Hirt, Stephen.............	42		13, 10, 7, 3		Luth.
Auckland, Arnold.... .....:	42		11, 9, 5, ¾	9	"
Wendels, Johan Peter......	42		10	3	"
Frank, Johan Martin.......	27				"
CARPENTERS					
Koster, Henry.............	51	wife	17, 13	10, 6	Luth.
Bertshy, Rudolph..........	24				Ref.
Gedert, Johan.............	26				Luth.
Wolfschlager, Melchoir.....	28				Cath.
Schmidt, Caspar..........	27				Luth.
Rottenflohr, John..........	36	wife	7	10	Cath.
Ehrenwein, John..........	30	"		2	"
Hafer, Peter..............	23				Luth.
Menges, John.............	35	wife	9, 3, ¼		Ref.
Dietrich, Bernhard.........	24				Luth.
Eisen, Anton..............	30	wife		5	Cath.
Schlecht, John.............	25	"		2	Ref.
Gnaedig, John.............	40	"	11, 5	1	Cath.
Escheroeder, Hendrick.....	46	"	18		Luth.
Conrad, Matthew..........	21				Cath.
Port, John.................	23				"
Lang, Christian...........	37	wife	5	11, 9, 2	"
Wickert, Melchoir.........	21				Luth.
Huper, Ludolf.............	24				Cath.
Schwarz, George..........	44	wife		13, 6, 3, 1 m.	Ref.
Knichel, John.............	27				Luth.
Metz, Andrew.............	40	wife	10, 5, 2	13	Ref.
Schlick, Martin...........	36	"			Cath.
Kniddelmeyer, Caspar......	25				"
Metz, Andrew.............	28	wife			Luth.
Dorry, Conrad.............	36				Cath.
Spad, Ludwig.............	30				"
Rufner, Thomas...........	28				Luth.
Gerhard, Peter............	32	wife			Cath.
Wolf, Conrad.............	32	"	1		Ref.
Schneider, Conrad.........	30	"	½	3	Luth.
Volldrauer, Matthew.......	34	"	15, 9, 8	4, 1	Cath.
Kuntz, Philip.............	22				Ref.
Kegelman, Leonhard.......	35	wife	9	6	"
Graef, Georg.............	30	"	½	4	Luth.
Bergman, Andreas.........	32	"		3	"
Lineman, Justus...........	26				Ref.
Buss, John Jacob..........	25				Luth.
Vier, Jacob................	26				
Drap, Lorentz.............	50	wife	13, 9, 3	10, 8, 4	Cath.
Noll, Bernhard.	47	"			Ref.
Habigt, John..............	50	"	9	6	Luth.
Black, Nicol..............	25	"			Ref.
Eydicker, John...........	23				Cath.
BAKERS					
Jacobi, John (will turn Protestant).................	45	wife	18, 12, 11, 6, 2	15, 8, ½	Cath.
Kraemer, John............	30	"		2	"

NAME	AGE	WIFE	SONS	DAUS.	CHURCH
Lanbegeier, Gottlieb.......	26				Luth.
Reif, John Peter............	64				Ref.
Hamel, John...............	66	wife	26		"
Lesch, John........	25	"	10, 6, 4, 5 ds.		Luth.
Wollebe, John..............	33	"	8, 5	10, 4, 1	Ref.
Wickhart, Conrad..........	31	"	4, 2	2	Luth.
Kloetter, John..............	29	"	1		Ref.
Hamel, Jonas..............	24				"
Dienes, August.............	26	wife			Cath.
TAILORS					
Barrabam, Ezechias........	30	wife			Ref.
Beck, Conrad..............	53	"			Cath.
Zacharias, Lorentz.........	47	"	12, 10	23,21,14,3	Luth.
Corrier, Carl..............	31	"			Cath.
Herber, Caspar............	48	"			Luth.
Warnon, Jacob.............	40	"	1	4	Cath.
Fisher, John..............	23	"	3		Luth.
Petri, Jacob...............	42	"	16, 10	19,15,12,5	"
Liebler, John..............	19				Cath.
Horst, Walter.............	39	wife	5	9, 3	Luth.
Spanknebel, Peter..........	19				Ref.
Umbauer, Adam...........	20				"
Wiesenegger, Caspar.......	24				Luth.
Conradt, Christoph.........	18				Ref.
Eydecker, Michel..........	16				Cath.
Weber, Valentin..........	31	wife	2		Ref.
Spader, Simon...	20				"
Alberts, Jacob.............	20				"
SHOEMAKERS					
Lichte, John..............	40	wife		5, 2	Ref.
Rab, Kilian..............	47	"	10, 7, 2		"
Diel, Adolf...............	32	"			"
Volk, Peter..............	29	"	6, 5, 1		Luth.
Volk, Oswald.............	27				"
Mekes, Bartin.............	31				"
Meic, Andrew.............	30				"
LaMothe, Daniel..........	30	wife	4	9, 1	"
Lerner, Matthew..........	50	"	9	8	Ref.
Gaus, Nicol..............	23				Luth.
Eich, Martin..............	29	wife	11	14,6,3,1	Cath.
Bay, Wendell.............	38	"	9, 4	13, 5, 3	Luth.
Kraft, Matthew............	37	"	12,6	8, 2	Cath.
Weiler, Andrew...........	45	"	7, 5, ½		Ref.
Weiss, Philip.............	44	"	20	18, 11, 9, 7,4	Luth.
Schiler, Matthew..........	36	"	6, 4, 1	7	Cath.
Heisterbach, Nicol.........	52	"	3	7, 5	Ref.
Doettel, John..............	22				Cath.
Spielman, John............	33				"
Roethgen, Nicol...........	20				Ref.
MASONS AND STONE CUTTERS					
Munkenast, Joseph.........	27	wife			Cath.
Trip, Matthew............	30	"	2	4	"
Halgarde, Peter...........	24				"
Blank, Cassran............	28				"
Waldman, Balzar.........	24				Luth.

NAME	AGE	WIFE	SONS	DAUS.	CHURCH
Egler, Christian...	28	wife	2	8, 7, 4	Ref.
Tragsal, Jacob.............	43	"	15	13, 11, 3	Cath.
Glaser, Dietrich............	26	"	4	6, ½	"
Master, Lambert...........	50	"	25	15	"
Los, Adam.................	21				Luth.
Los, John.................	40	wife	7	11	Cath.
Zick, Conrad..............	21				"
Roethgen, Peter...........	27	wife	1		Ref.
Krochner, John............	40	"	18		Cath.
Schoepf, Thomas..........	40	"			"
Schmidt, Henry............	48	"	19, 15, 6	21; 15	Ref.
Theis, Thomas.............	30	"	1		Cath.
Roeger, Dietrich...........	32				"
Lopp, Jacob...............	40	wife	7, 1 m.	5, 4	Luth.
Weimar, Simon............	30				Cath.
Wolfee, Peter.............	30	wife			"
Mulleker, Francis..........	30	"	1		"
Trausch, John.............	18				Luth.
Isler, Nicholas............	48	wife	15, 8, 6	5, 1	Ref.
MASONS					
Reideman, Martin..........	24				Cath.
Gerger, John..............	31				"
Mueller, Georg............	26				Luth.
Lunch, Caspar............	37	wife		7, 2	"
JOYNERS					
Zimmerman, Matthew......	38	wife	9, 6		Ref.
Naegler, Jacob............	30				"
Koster, Dietrich...........	36	wife	11	6, 3	Luth.
Rufer, Peter..............	19				Ref.
Ditmar, David.............	22				Luth.
Menges, John.............	32	wife			"
Weber, Michael...........	50	"	18, 13		Cath.
Scheman, Valentin........	25				Ref.
HUNTERS					
Lambrecht, Georg..........	44	wife	20, 16, 14, 7	17, 9	Luth.
Bundersgell, John..........	36	"	4	9, 7, 2	Cath.
Goeddel, Jacob............	60	"	20, 16, 14	10, 4, 2	Luth.
BUTCHERS					
Giees, Fridrik.............	42	wife	4	10, 2	Ref.
Andrus, Michel...........	30	"		2	"
Diess, John..............	30	"			Cath.
Marry, David.............	40	"	10, 2	8 days	Ref.
Munchofer, Philipp........	36	"			Cath.
Ashenburg, William........	40	"		3	Luth.
Schomberger, Georg.......	31	"			Ref.
du Bray, Peter............	19				"
LINEN WEAVERS					
Slott, Ulrich..............	43	wife	17, 9	11	Cath.
Kern, Francis.............	30	"		6, 2	"
Miller, Philip.............	23				Ref.
Dietz, William............	33	wife		1	"
Schnaeblin, Rudolf........	30	"	3, ¾	6	"
Merket, Peter.............	38	"	4		"
Schafer, John.............	29	"	4, 2, ¼	5	Cath.
Rhode, Philip.............	34	"	2 m.	19, 14, 4	Ref.

NAME	AGE	WIFE	SONS	DAUS.	CHURCH
Hach, Peter................	35	wife		2	Ref.
Hochappel, John...........	43	"	23, 16, 10	12, 4	"
Artus, Isac................	43	"			"
Heyd, Nicol...............	24				Cath.
Koehler, Jacob............	54	wife	16, 10, ½	18, 14, 12, 10, 4	Luth.
Wickhart, William.........	23				"
Mahler, Bastian...........	24	wife			Cath.
Land, Anton...............	26	"		1	"
Aldenuess, Philip..........	43	"	9, 4	7	Luth.
Kreisher, Ludwig..........	24				"
Ringer, John Thiel........	24				"
Hanson, Bernhard.........	32	wife	12, 4	9, 1	Cath.
Gesch, Godfried...........	37	"	3		Luth.
Schwan, John.............	25				"
Big, John.................	24				Ref.
Dietrich, Jacob...........	44	wife	18, 12, 2	15,12,10,6	"
Walter, Rudolf............	28	"	15, 8		"
Scherer, Just..............	76				"
Rehm, Anton..............	41	wife	3	2	Cath.
COOPERS AND BREWERS					
Friedrik, Nicol............	60	wife	25, 21	17, 15	Luth.
Alman, Simon.............	25				"
Reiser, Michel............	24				Ref.
Stricksheiser, Balzar.......	45	wife	9	13, 5	"
That, Bernhard...........	45	"	6	2	Luth.
Meyer, Jacob.............	20				"
Bruch, Michael...........	27				"
Frank, Michel............	20				Cath.
Frantz, Conrad............	20				Ref.
Tanner, Urban............	33	wife		6, 4, 3, 1	
Kemmer, Peter...........	28	"			Luth.
Metzger, Philip...........	40	"	13,10,7, ¼	9, 4	"
Herman, Philip............	25	"			"
Hardtz, John..............	30				Cath.
Behler, Henry............	30				Ref.
Zeller, John...............	23				Luth.
Kaul, Matthew............	50	wife	16,14,10,8	5, 2	Ref.
Braun, Lucas.............	32	"	1	6	"
Mara, Peter...............	24				Cath.
Kirches, Paul.............	23				"
Ehrlich, John.............	25				Ref.
Muller, Adam.............	36	wife	8	12, 6	"
Merden, Christoph........	40	"	8, ¼	12, 6	"
TURNERS					
Schneider, Joachim........	41	wife		13, 11, 4	Ref.
Faber (Taber), Ebert......	20				Luth.
MILLERS					
Meier, Paul...............	43	wife	12, 7	13, 8, ½	Luth.
Schmidt, Matthew.........	30	"	5, 3		Cath.
Hofman, Henry...........	33	"		6, 3, 1	Luth.
Herling, Conrad...........	28				"
Christhiles, George........	28	wife	¼		Cath.
Pfeifer, Peter.............	57	"	19, 5		Luth.
Kraus, John Michel........	50		24, 6		"
Mungesser, Philip..........	27	wife	6	1 ¼	"
Weiss, George.............	20				Ref.

NAME	AGE	WIFE	SONS	DAUS.	CHURCH
SMITHS					
Meiss, Henry..............	38	wife	3, ¼		Ref.
Wagner, Conrad...........	46	"	15,12,11,9	7, 5	Luth.
Schezinger, John...........	37	"	5		Cath.
Bauer, John................	22				Luth.
Ruhl, Daniel...............	24				Ref.
Sherer, Peter..............	26				Luth.
Becker, Michel.............	24	wife			"
Shmidt, Nicol..............	46	"	18, 9	9, 12, 10	"
Giessiebel, John Michel,....	28	"		2	"
Fuchs, John Bernhard......	39	"	9, 5, 2	7	Cath.
Carp, John.................	50	"	14, 12	22, 17, 7	Luth.
Albert, John...............	23				Ref.
Scheur, Peter...............	22				Cath.
Bast, Nicol................	50	wife	23, 21, 2	18, 15, 13, 12, 8	Ref.
Steinbacher, Philip.........	30	"	2		Luth.
WOOLEN WEAVERS					
Weichel, Frederick........	30	wife	2		Ref.
Hollander, Melchoir........	20				Luth.
STOCKING WEAVERS					
Schmidt, Peter......	36	wife	8	12,10,3, ½	Ref.
Michel, Henry.............	38			6	Luth.
TANNERS					
Fohrer, John...............	60	wife	20, 18		Cath.
Hess, Andrew..............	24				Ref.
SADDLERS					
Winter, Melchior...........	42	wife	5		Cath.
Petri, Andrew..............	39	"		9, 6, 4	Ref.
WHEELWRIGHTS					
Schmidt, Michel...........	55		23, 21,12, 8	25	Luth.
Philipps, Jacob.............	19				"
Henrich, Caspar...........	24				Cath.
Gresman, Henry...........	28				Luth.
Manke, George.............	20				Ref.
POTTERS					
Mehden, Martin............	42	wife	10, 7, 4	14, 7	Cath.
Meyer, Egidy..............	22				"
Walter, Jacob..............	16				Ref.
TILE					
Wannenmacher, Henry.....	64	wife	20		Cath.
BRICKMAKERS					
Carten, John..............	46	wife	20, 14, 11	9, 6, 2	Luth.
du Bray, John..............	26	"	4, 2		Ref.
SURGEONS					
Bucholts, John.............	30				Luth.
Rhod, Jacob...............	44	wife	8	2	Cath.
FIGUREMAKER					
Legoli, John...............	26	wife	1		Ref.
LOCKSMITH					
Herbst, John...............	46	wife	5	3	Cath.

NAME	AGE	WIFE	SONS	DAUS.	CHURCH
HATTER					
Hopf, George..............	38	wife			Luth.
MINERS					
Pfiz, Joseph................	33	wife	6, 2		Luth·
Pfiz, Jacob................	30				"
WIDOWS					
Zinckin, Elizabeth..........	26		2	6, 3	Luth.
Wenzelin, Anne............	47				Cath,
Mullerin, Mary.............	30			8, 6	Ref.
Meyerin, Barbara..........	60			18	Luth.
Rosmanin, Catherin........	54			20	"
Finkin, Ursula.............	46		9	19	Cath.
Wellerin, Anna............	38		7, 2		Ref.
Mullerin, Mary.............	30			8, 6	"
Meyerin, Barbara..........	60			18	Luth.
Seelingerin, Margretha.....	54				Ref.
Rutigin, Elizabeth..........	60				Cath.
Hay, Eva..................	30			1	Ref.
Andelsin, Catherin........	50				·Cath.
Keinin, Rose........	50		19		Ref.
Ekern, Anna..............	44		9		Luth.
Schneiderin, Margretha.....	30			7	Ref.
Sonnenhofin, Mary.........	60				"
Keyserin, Anna............	30				Cath.
Noset, Susana.............	60				"
Lescherin, Magdalen.......	34		18		Ref.
Mathesin, Anna............	53			23, 20, 18	"
Bodin, Mary..............	50			24, 22, 12	"
Wenzel, Anna Mary........	50				Luth.
Schuch, Anna Catherine....	64				Ref.
Schmid, Christine..........	60				"
Schaeferin, Eleanore.......	45				Luth.
Sickin, Cecelia.............	26		6		Ref.
Jaegerin, Elizabeth.........	70				"
Nellesin, Anna Eve........	50		16	11	"
Huntin, Jane..............	60		30		Cath.
Meyschin, Jane............	36			2	Luth.
Schwart, Jane Jacob.			13, 9	7, 14, 2	Ref.
Jungin, Elizabeth..........	45				"
Schmid, Barbara...........	22		2		"
Kueferin, Eva.............	25		8	6	Cath.
Muellerin, Susanna........	32				Ref.
Herzin, Margretha........	50		16, 10	14, 7	Cath.
Engels, Anna Mary........	60				Ref.
Nonin, Elizabeth...........	60				"
Volpertin, Margretha.......	45			26	"
Slacyrin, Elizabeth.........	23			5	"
Hup, Margretha...........	30		8	11, 6, 4	"
Fischerin, Margretha.......	55				Cath.
Altheim, Anna.............	64				Luth.
Schellberger, Catherine.....	34		1	5	Ref.
Meyshin, Anna.............	30			2	Luth.
Schwartz, Elizabeth........	40		13, 9	7, 2	"
UNMARRIED WOMEN					
Tauflin, Catherine..........	20				Ref.
Tagin, Catherine..........	30				Luth.
Forsterin, Anna............	20				Ref.
Fuchsin, Mary.............	22				Luth.
Fuchsin, Margareth........	18				"

NAME	AGE	WIFE	SONS	DAUS.	CHURCH
Bergin, Anna...............	25				Ref.
Weidmannin, Elizabeth....	21				"
Zeltnerin, Urzula...........	20				"
Ozeberger, Mary...........	18				Cath.
Hey, Anna.................	18				Ref.
Durrin, Catherine..........	30				Cath.
Appelin, Elizabeth.........	30				"
Rup, Margretha............	16				Ref.
Jaegerin, Mary............	18				Cath.
Meyerin, Elizabeth.........	30				Luth.
Gott, Mary................	38				Ref.
Huberin, Christina.........	21				"
Manderset, Mary...........	26				Cath.
Schmidt, Eva Mary........	17				"
Lutz, Anna Mary...........	20				"
Brugerin, Mary............	19				Luth.
Muserin, Anna.............	24				"
Lauer, Agnes..............	20				Cath.
Henzelin, Eva.............	21				"
Henzelin, Mary............	23				"
Margareth, Elizabeth.......	18				"
Jahnin, Elizabeth..........	19				"
Volkerin, Margareth........	20				Luth.
Closin, Mary,..............	30				"
Margretha, Anna...........	15				"
Geldmacherin, Sabina......	21				"
Hubnerin, Margaret........	20				Cath.
'Hoffman. Catherin.........	24				"
Bellin, Mary...............	21				Ref.
Midler, Juliana............	21				"
Eyfelin, Christina.........	20				Cath.
Witschlager, Magdalene....	25				"
Haas, Elizabeth...........	21				Ref.
Langin, Elizabeth..........	22				Cath.
Dales, Catherine..........	25				Ref.
Fishers, Margaretha........	24				Cath.
Burder, Magdalena........	22				Ref.
Mullerin, Margaretha......	23				Cath.
Laurmannin, Eva..........	22				Ref.
Mallot, Catharina..........	20				Cath.
Kahl, Margaretha..........	31				Ref.
Fischerin, Margaretha......	55				Cath.
Glasin, Margaretha........	21				"
Catherin, Anna............	16				"
Dres, Catherine............	19				"

LIST.

Schooolmasters................	5	Turners........................	2
Husbandmen & Vinedressers ...	460	Millers........................	9
Carpenters....................	45	Smiths........................	15
Bakers.......................	11	Wheelwrights..................	5
Tailors......................	18	Woolen Weavers...............	2
Shoemakers	20	Stocking Weavers..............	2
Masons......................	28	Tanners.......................	2
Joiners......................	8	Saddlers......................	2
Butchers..................	8	Hunters.......................	3
Linenweavers.......	27	Potters.......................	3
Coopers	23	Brickmakers..................	3

Total, 590

(Endorsed) Miscellanies List of Poor Palatines arrived from Germany 2. June, 1709. Received from Mr. Rupert, 21 Juue, 1709. D. 68.

LISTS OF GERMANS FROM THE PALATINATE WHO CAME TO ENGLAND IN 1709.

The following lists are copied from the original documents preserved in the British Museum Library, London, England, and should be of the greatest genealogical interest to those families in the States of New York, New Jersey, Pennsylvania and elsewhere, which claim descent from the so-called Palatine settlers. These lists have never before been printed to the knowledge of the Editor, and it should be noted that the word "son" or "sons" and "dau." or "daus." followed by figures denote that the heads of the family had as many sons or daughters, as there are figures, and that these sons and daughters were of the respective ages denoted by the figures. The word "wife" indicates that the head of the family was married and that the wife was living. The abbreviations "Ref.," "Luth.,' "Bap." and "Cath.," mean that the family belonged to the Reformed, Lutheran, Baptist or Catholic Churches.

BOARD OF TRADE MISCELLANIES. VOL. 2. NOS. D 69 & D 70.

PUBLIC RECORD OFFICE, LONDON.

BOARD OF TRADE MISCELLANIES. VOL. 2, D 69.

List of poor Palatines who arrived at St. Cathrin's, June 11th, 1709, taken at St. Catherine's and Debtford, June 15.

NAME	AGE	WIFE	SONS	DAUS.	CHURCH
HUSBANDMEN & VINEDRESSERS					
Schnorr, Nicol............	50	wife	12	22, 17	Luth.
Baehr, Nicol..............	52	"	18		Ref.
Keller, Jacob.............	58	"	4		"
Liris (Siris), Martin........	40	"	¼	12,11,10, 4	Luth.
Mueller, Jacob............	50	"	6	14	Ref.
Hank, Bleigart............	46	"	7	4	"
Ledig, Nicol............ ...	25	"	2 weeks	1½	"
Biederman, John..........	48	"			"
Zolker, Balzar.............	70	sing.			"
Helfrich, Henrich.........	50	wife	19, 16		"
Lechner, Michel..........	40	"	14, 3		Cath.
Wingart, John.............	46	"	18, 13, 11, 8, 6		Bapt.
Wiehelm, Mathes..........	40	"	23, 15, 11		Ref.
Rappell, John.............	32	"		4	
Leib, John...............	43	"	10	14, ½	Ref.
Mess, Abraham........	34	"		14, 2	
Herzel, Adam.............	44	"		14	Luth.
Zerbst, Peter.............	50	"	24	28, 27, 25, 23, 14	Cath.
Resch, Adam.............	50	"	17, 11,6	19, 18	
Maur, John.............	36	"	13,11.10, 3	½	
Kuehn, Herman..........	55	"	26	28, 18	Cath.
Peder, Nicol.............	40	"	16,15, 9, 2	8	"
Krutsch, John.............	40	"	2	8, 6, 4	"

NAME	AGE	WIFE	SONS	DAUS.	CHURCH
Bork, Henrich..............	50	wife		20, 12, 4	
Doenny, Martin............	44	"	6	16	Cath.
Herman, Justus............	41	"		14, 7	Luth.
Becker, John..............	30	"		3, 1	Cath.
Hofman, Philip............	30	"	1		Luth.
Bork, Matthes.............	40	"	13, 11, 2	10, 8, 5	Cath.
Tielman, Conrad...........	30	"	8, 6, 1½	9	"
Steiner, Michel............	50	"			"
Schutz, Martin.............	22	"	½		"
Metzger, John.............	32	"		1½	"
Graner, Jacob.............	60	sing.			Ref.
Buntz, Nicol..........:	30	wife	16	14, 8	Cath.
Meyer, Paulus.............	18	"			"
Scheuer, John.............	35	"			"
Engel, William...........	27	"			"
Mutz, Friederik...........	22	"			"
Schueler, Peter...........	46	"	7, 1	20, 14, 5	"
Sontag, Francis...........	36	"	5, 1	13, 5	"
Engler, Peter.............	30	"	5	2	"
Borr, Matthes.............	45	"	21	18	"
Schunger, Theobald........	38	"	13, 11, 5	2	"
Creutz, Matthes...........	40	"	18, 7, 6, 2	9, 4	"
Creutz, John..............	36	"	13	10, 7	"
Schmidt, Caspar...........	30	"	2		Ref.
Ludwig, Henry............	40	"	18, 10		Luth.
Keusel, Jacob.............	44	"	7, 1½	13, 11	"
Mueller, Martin...........	32	"	8, 6, 5	2	Ref.
Lang, Wolf...............	30	"	1	6, 3	Cath.
Schoepfer, George........	32	"			Ref.
Ulrich, Elias.............	46	"	8	13, 2½	"
Rosbach, Peter...........	40	"	12, 7		Luth.
Rennersbacher, Christian...	24	"			Ref.
Herman, Sebastian........	26	"			"
Mansbeil, Caspar..........	33	"	5		Luth.
Kurtz, George.............	37	"	12		"
Fritz, Nicol..............	54	"	20, 14, 13, 9	15, 11, 2	Cath.
Reischardt, Christian.......	32	"	3	4	Ref.
Meyer, Adam..............	30	"			Cath.
Heibel, Bernhardt.........	40	"	8	14, 3, 1	Ref.
Gro, George..............	40	"	2	7, 5	Luth.
Gro, Philip..............	30	"	6, 5, 3, 1		"
Stengel, Philip.............	54	sing.			"
Rink, Melchior............	42	wife	16	10	Ref.
Walter, Caspar...........	44	"	21, 16, 12, 8, 4	18, 14, 12, 6	Luth.
Schales, Peter............	38	"		15, 12, 4	Ref.
Baum, Abraham.	34	"	14, 12, 3, 1	15	
Schmidt, Peter...........	33	"	12, 10	14, 2	Ref.
Hodel, Isaac..........	36	"	¼		"
Eschweilen, Thomas.......	34	"		10, 6	"
Eschwein, Jacob..........	41	"	15	7, 1	"
Zepp, Leonhardt..........	44	"	20, 19, 8	17	"
Mengel, Wendel..........	27	"	3	5, 2 days	"
Brathecker, Justus........	44			18, 11, 9, 3, 1	
Schaefer, Zerben..........	40	wife	12		Cath.
Coblentzer, John..........	28	"	5	2	Ref.
Christman, John..........	4?	"	7, 5	9, 2	Mennon
Kintig, John..............	4?	"	12, 10	17, 16, 6	Ref
Hedgen, Conrad........ ..	??	"	17		"
Krenig, John.............	4?	"	?		

NAME	AGE	WIFE	SONS	DAUS.	CHURCH
Batz, Friedrich............	28	wife	5, 3	8	Luth.
Crabbecher, Peter..........	28	"	2		"
Tachfletter, George.........	30	"	3		"
Seip (Leip), Michel........	23	"			"
Speicherman, Herman..... .	46	"	16	18	"
Boll, Caspar..............	40	"		4	"
Morheiser, Nicol.........:..	26	"	7	2	Cath.
Matthes, Lorentz...........	75		24		Luth.
Brunwasser, Herman.......	31	wife	1		"
Schwed, Jacob.............	42	"	18, 13, 8	10, 5, 4, ¼	Cath.
Binhammer, Barthel........	37	"	6, 1	10, 3	"
Lutz, John...............	33	"	10, 7, 3	14	Ref.
Peter, Jacob..............	22	"			"
Bachler, Michel...........	47	"	5	12, 10, 7	"
Hupfer, David............	30	"		12, 9	"
Hern, John..............	37	"	7, 5	2	"
Weber, Dietrich...........	42	"	1	15	Cath.
Vorbeck, John.............	56	"		½	"
Eilen, Henry..............	38	"	12, 8, 3		"
Pommer, Bongraf..........	45		17	14	"
Stegen, Nicol..............	58	wife	7, 3	14, 12	Luth.
Schleicher, George.........	40	"	3	19, 17, 1	"
Hagadorn, Peter...........	60	"	24, 22, 15	17, 11	"
Salbach, John.............	52	"		17, 14	"
Sahlbach, Edmund.........	21	"			"
Fuchs, John...............	30	"	4, 1		"
Propfer, Justus............	30	"	7, 4	9	"
Balzar, Jacob.....	40	"	9, 6	15	Cath.
Thiel, John...............	50	"		18, 12	Luth.
Tiel, Herman..............	26	"		2	"
Ess, Jacob................	49	"		1	Cath.
Wend, Henry..............	38	"	15, 5, 2	10	Luth.
Bitter, Jacob..............	31	"	10, 5, ½		"
Bakus, Ferdinand..........	31	"	4	2	Cath.
Stott, Dietrich.............	31	"		4	"
Dietrich, Nicol.............	46	"	17, 10, 5, 2	18, 15, 7	"
Beyer, Thomas............	28	"		6, 4, 2	Luth.
Fischer, Peter.............	36	"		5, 2	Ref.
Busch, Daniel.............	65	"			"
Meyer, Henry.............	43	"	4	6	"
Pulver, Wendel...........	30	"	5, 2		Cath.
Wilmar, Anton............	40	"	13		Luth.
Eberhard, Michel..........	44	"	21, 12, 8	13	Ref.
Mueller, Henry............	34	"	4, 3	1	"
Kuhns, Conrad............	44	"	24	20	Luth.
Gesner, Conrad............	26	"	2, ½		"
Schaefer, Andreas..........	50	"	27, 24, 17	20	"
Sorg, Matthes..............	54	"	4	10, 7	Cath.
Paul, Henry...............	50	"	21, 7, 5	17, 14, 12, 9	Luth.
Sperling, Peter............	47	"	10, 8, 4	18, 16, 14	"
Kaefer, Casimir...........	23	"			"
Schintzerling, John.	41	"		12, 8, 4	Ref.
Rup, Peter................	42	"	20, 16	14, 12, 2	"
Berger, John..............	45	"	16, 14, 8	20, 10	"
Nuss, Ludwig.............	46	"		15, 12, 10	"
Oberdubbel, Jacob.........	35	"	4, 2	11	Cath.
Kesler, George.....	40	"	14, 10, 6, 3		"
Wolpert, Nicol.............	30	"	10	10, 6, 3	"
Engel, John...............	36	"			"
Borkes, Herman...........	25	"	1, ¼		"
Themer, John.............	36	"	15, 11, 8, 6	1	Luth.

NAME	AGE	WIFE	SONS	DAUS.	CHURCH
Ehresman, Michel........	46	wife	20	22, 13, 7	Ref.
Johann, Nicol.............	32	"	13, 9, 7	6, 1	Luth.
Laekman, Isaac............	36	"	10	7, 4	Ref.
Schreiner, Simon..........	36	"	4, 2	12, 10, 8	Cath.
Lauer, John..............	27	"		7, 6, 3	"
Daniel, Anton.............	40	"	17, 12, 6, 1	18, 8, 4	"
Mitwig, Germanus........	54	"	18	14	"
Baum, Fridrik.............	45	"	14	21, 19, 15	"
Wind, Peter..............	41	"	21, 8, 7, 2	18	"
Volks, Arnold.............	32	"	9, 1	13, 4	"
Schmidt, Nicol............	36	"	12		Ref.
Froebus, George..........	39	"	18	20, 12	"
Schmidt, Nicol...........	19	"			"
Emmel, Christoph.........	27	"	7	3	"
Kesseler, Caspar..........	65		20	25	Cath.
Sottig, Herman...........	40	wife	11, 7	14, 9, 5	"
Bestel, Jacob........	33	"			"
Becker, John.............	26	"		1½	"
Lorentz, Dietrich.........	34	"	12, 3		"
(L.?) Sinnenbaum, Peter....	50	"	20, 3, 1		"
Schneider, Ulrich.........	34(?)	"	24(?), 1		Ref.
Schmidt, Adam.............	36	"		13, 10, 8	Cath.
Hilles, Nicol.............	40	"	10	16, 13, 5	Ref.
Fuchs, George.............	40	"	12	17, 10, 8, 6	Cath.
Dressel, John.............	32	"		1	"
Schmidt, John.............	35	"	8	3, ¼	"
Lennebaum, Christoph.....	26	"		4, 2	"
Wicked, Bernhard........	36	"	11, 5, ½	8	"
Staut, Grin...............	30	"			Ref.
Mohr, Augustin............	36	"	13, 4, 2	6	Cath.
Autlen, Paulus............	39	"	17, 9, 6, 3	12	"
Roemer, John.............	26	"	1	3	"
Lerne, Matthes...........	42	"	15, 12, 2	14, 8	"
Leophard, John............	38	"	7, 3	14, 12, 7	"
Guck, John	35	"		3	"
Alten, John..............	56	"		23, 22, 9, 4	"
Lenacker, Peter...........	36	"	14, 9, 6	14, 12, 10, 7, 2	"
Leich, Simon.............	34	"	6	1½	Luth.
Heins, John Adam..........	33	"	6		"
Heins, Nicol.	24	"	1		"
Gross, Dietrich...........	27	"			Cath.
Getman, Caspar...........	36	"	16, 14, 8, 5	6, 5, 2	Luth.
Gross, William............	56	"	12, 9	5	Cath.
Valentins, Velten..........	20	"			Cath.
Kulpfaber, Jacob...........	26	"		4, 2	Ref.
Gebel, Henrich..	24	"	12, 10	14, 2	Luth.
Schmids, Henry...........	60		15, 12		
Schenkel, John............	44	wife	10	13, 8, 5	Ref.
Valentin, John............	56	"	14, 3	16, 8	Cath.
Arnold, Philip.............	30	"		5, 3	"
Volhart, John.............	30	"	20, 18, 15	13, 12	Luth.
Schmidt, John............	35	"	8	3, ¼	Cath.
Mueller, Peter............	45	"	18, 6, 4		"
Fris, John................	30	"	7, 2	8, 5	"
Metz, Sebastian...........	36	"	18	15, 7	Luth.
Mumenthal, Jacob.........	48	"			Ref.
Schmidt, Arnd.............	30		10	3	"
Herich, Jost..............	50	"	16, 11, 7	18, 12, 5	Cath.
Braun, Nicol.............	60	"	20, 15, 11	17, 8, 1	Ref.

NAME	AGE	WIFE	SONS	DAUS.	CHURCH
Hauch, Lucas...............	31(?)	wife	22(?), 16, 13, 9, 3, 8 days	13, 12, 9	Ref.
Becker, John...............	28	"			Luth.
Mullen, Gerhard...........	35	"	7		Cath.
Ermitter, Francis..........	35	"	7	5, 2	"
Schumacher, Bartel........	41	"	11, 6	17, 14, 8	Luth.
Bellesheim, Peter..........	27	"	1		Cath.
Fehling, Henry............	24	"			Ref.
Krantz, Conrad............	23	"		1	"
Sherner, John Michel.......	39	"	7, 3	18,16,14, 4	Luth.
Schmidt, George...........	53	"	22, 20, 2	18,16,14, 8	"
Reuter, Ludwig............	32	"			Ref.
Zerbst, Martin............	34	"	11, 8, 4, 2		Luth.
Mullen, Michael...........	26	"	2	1	"
Michel, Nichol............	30	"			"
Bartel, Henrich............	45	"	17, 14, 9	20, 6	"
Stoss, John................	40	"	10, 1	16, 3	Cath.
Giss, Jost.................	39	"	12, 10, 3	5	"
Saar, John.................	50	"	20, 18, 5, 5, 2	14, 9	"
Huhn, Henry..............	48				Ref.
Faber, Adam..............	30				"
Kludy, George.............	22				"
Wilhelm, Paul.............	30				"
Son, Philip................	30				"
Cleman, Peter.............	17				Luth.
Reichardt, Valentin........	18				Cath.
Friede, Nicol..............	21				Luth.
Biss, Nicol................	20				Cath.
Stin, Titius...............	20				"
Baus, Nicol................	24				"
Knauer, Zacharias.........	26				Ref.
Busch, Justus.............	24				Luth.
Schwab, Philip............	20				Ref.
Peters, John..............	19				Cath.
Seibel, Valentin...........	22				Ref.
Seibel, George............	20				"
Wilhelm, John............	40				"
Riegel, Christian..........	20				Cath.
Geibel, Peter..............	17				Luth.
Schnick, Michel...........	22				Ref.
Heller, Wolf..............	26				Luth.
Ehrenbach, Michel........	27				"
Valentin, Henry...........	20				Cath.
Burger, Caspar............	26				"
Dewick, Francis..........	22				"
Henning, Andreas.........	38				Ref.
Beckart, Christian.........	26				Cath.
Hohenfedd, Lorentz.......	22				"
Durr, Philipp.............	27				"
Dudenbecker, John........	18				Luth.
Omes, Peter..............	21				Cath.
Reuter, Nicol.............	25				"
Christ, John...............	20				"
Reuter, Ludwig...........	14				"
Gamben, John............	24				"
Vogt, Henry..	25				Ref.
Wenckel, Henry...........	23				Cath.
Drosel, William...........	36				Ref.
Hensel, Valentine.........	20				"

NAME	AGE	WIFE	SONS	DAUS.	CHURCH
Schuster, Peter............	40				Cath.
Zerbst, Conrad............	39				Ref.
COOPERS					
Tieffenbach, Conrad........	50	wife		11, 4, 1	Ref.
Leasch, Burchard..........	28	"			Luth.
Kirsch, Adam.............	28	"	6	2, ¼	Cath.
Leis, Matthes.............	38	"	12, ½	18, 16, 11, 8, 7	"
Tiel, Jacob...............	24				Luth.
Frantzberg, John..........	24				"
Ganter, Christian..........	50	wife	4	20, 1	Ref.
Heiden, Jacob.............	44	"	1		"
Schoemacher, Michel.......	24				Luth.
Ziegler, Andreas..........	40	wife		3, 1	Ref.
Baum, Friederich..........	45	"	14	21, 19, 15	Cath.
Buch, Henry..............	49	"	17	24, 16, 12, 3	"
CARPENTERS					
Klein, William............	26	wife			Luth.
Margart, Peter............	50	"	24		Cath.
Kless, John..............	28	"		3	"
Rosing, Matthas..........	23				"
Weber, Sebastian.........	30				Ref.
Weber, Henry.............	24				"
Schummer, John..........	20				Cath.
Siffer, Bastian...........	21	wife			Ref.
Metz, Simon.............	33	"	4	7, 2	Cath.
Blatz, Andreas...........	32	"	2	5	Luth.
Buchsel, Augustin........	50	"	25, 22, 20, 16, 12, 8, 1		Ref.
Schmidt, Peter...........	39	"	10	14, 5, 2	Cath.
Strosser, Daniel..........	60	"	12		Ref.
Scheyer, John............	30	"	3		"
Liset, Philip.............	24	"			"
Luich, Kostman...........	36	"	22, 8		"
Wadenspfhul, Jacob.......	32	"	3, 1		Luth.
Gerser, Henry...........	36	"	7, 4	13, 10	"
Thalheimer, Nicol.........	27	"		3, 1	"
Schezel, Jacob............	39	"			"
Bauer, Christoph..........	21				"
Jung, Nicol..............	21				"
MASONS					
Closs, Simon.............	26	wife		½	Cath.
Mauer, George............	32				Luth.
Besler, Francis............	46	wife	18, 16, 7		Cath.
Moor, David.............	36	"			Ref.
Beus, Jacob..............	30	"	6, 1		Cath.
Carat, John	16				Ref.
Mey, John...............	36	wife	½	8, 6, 4	Cath.
JOINERS					
Son, Elias...............	21				Luth.
Pfhul, Peter.............	48	wife	10, 5, 1	12, 6	"
Gruber, Matthes..........	46	"	14, 12, 10, 4	1	Cath.
Julius, Henrich...........	21				Luth.
Koerner, John............	33				"
WHEELWRIGHTS					
Tiel, Ananias.............	36	wife	5, 1		Luth.
Hoges, Michel............	26				Cath.
Klein, Adam.............	28				Ref.

NAME	AGE	WIFE	SONS	DAUS.	CHURCH
SMITHS					
Deller, Jacob..............	22				Luth.
New, Wenceslag...........	20				Cath.
Meyer, George............	19				Luth.
Schmidt, Christian.........	18				Ref.
Kerber, Nicol.............	50	wife	¼		Cath.
Stein, William............	23				"
Klein, Philip..............	45	wife	9, 7	4	Ref.
Schmidt, Carl.............	36	"	10, 9, 7, 4	1	Luth.
Hohn, Michel.............	31	"	4	10, 4	"
Roll, Jost.................	26	"			Cath.
Schantz, Peter............	20				Luth.
Michel, John..............	42	wife			Cath.
LINEN AND CLOTH WEAVERS					
Brill, Michell..............	21				Cath.
Waller, John..............	49	wife			"
Forster, George...........	39	"		14, 10, 7, 5	Luth.
Kessler, Nicol.............	24	"			"
Muller, Anton.............	56	"			Ref.
Bless, Conrad.............	29	"			"
Wieser, Jacob.............	52	"	16		"
Boset, Daniel.............	59	"	14, 5	21, 19, 13, 11, 9, 1 m.	"
Herman, Sebastian........	36				Cath.
Kolhaus, Lucas...........	40	wife	3	11, 8	"
Barl, Henrich.............	54	"	22	18, 16, 14, 12	Ref.
Kuhn, Peter..............	24				Luth.
Maus, Michel.............	24				Cath,
Maus, Reinhard...........	18				"
Bock, Jacob..............	40				Ref.
TAILORS					
Reichard, Henry..........	15				Cath.
Ludwig, Anton............	28	wife	2	6	"
Brozis, Adam.............	33	"	1	4	"
Arlot, Francis.............	22				"
Ostwald, John............	44	wife	14, 3	22, 6	Luth.
Heddesheimer, Henry......	22				Ref.
Walten, John.............	20				"
Leilling (Salling?), Francis.	16				Cath.
Erlenbach, George........	53	wife	6	16, 8	Ref.
Wremmar, John..........	18				Cath.
Merzel, Jacob.............	30	wife			Luth.
Hag, Caspar..............	20				"
Forster, Nicol.............	22				Ref.
Schmidt, John Peter.......	19				Luth.
Schmidt, Peter...........	19				"
Klein (Lang?), Moritz.....	30	wife	8, 6	10, 4, 1	Cath.
SCHOOLMASTERS					
Regel, Matthes............	40	wife	2		Cath.
Kummer, John.............	40		9, 1	8, 6	Ref.
Rasor, Frederick..........	29				Luth.
SHOEMAKERS					
Decker, John..............	29	wife	½		Cath.
Ferry, John C.............	23	"			"
Pfalzer, Henry............	36	"	5, 2	10	"
Horsbach, Dietrich........	36	"	6	1	"

NAME	AGE	WIFE	SONS	DAUS.	CHURCH
Nusbaum, John............	46	wife	13, 9, 6, 2	17, 13	Mennon
Hen, Henrich	40	"	13, 11, 9, 6	2	Luth.
Albiger, William...........	34	"			"
Eckman, John,.............	36	"		4	
Munster, Peter.............	30	"	9, 4	8, 6	Luth.
Adams, Jacob..............	24	"			"
Reid, Nicol................	34	"	13	10	"
Gibstein, Martin...........	33				Cath.
BRICKLAYERS					
Maus, Dietrich.............	30	wife	9, 6	4	Cath.
Klepper, Conrad...........	33	"	9, 2	5	"
Horning, Gerhard..........	40	"		6, 2	Ref.
Hag, Henry................	26	"	3	1	Luth.
STOCKING WEAVERS					
Matthes, Mareus...........	88			24	Ref.
Matthas, George..........	32	wife	3		"
Michel, Henry.............	38	"	8, 5	10, 1	Luth.
BAKERS					
Schmidt, John..............	23	wife	3		Cath.
Brandau, William..........	30	"	3		Ref.
Schwab, Conrad............	20				Luth.
Kuhlbrunner, Caspar.......	23				Ref.
Brenner (Bronner), Balzar..	20				Luth.
Ganglof, John.............	28	wife		4 mos.	"
Shoemaker, John...........	37				Ref.
Meyer, Barthol.....	50	wife		14, 3, 6, 5	Luth.
Buerger, John...	55	"	12	20	Cath.
Lucerni, Abraham..........	27				Ref.
Roth, Andreas.............	24				Luth.
HUNTSMEN					
Reuter, Henry.............	34	wife		4, 2	Cath.
Gerlach, Conrad...........	49	"	7, 5	16, 11	Ref.
HATTERS					
Wegrauch, Valentin........	38	wife	7, 2	11, 9	Luth.
Andoit, Samuel............	44	"	20	13, 13	Ref.
GLAZIERS					
la Dour, John......	18				Cath.
Rose, Christoph............	35				Luth.
Meiss, Barthol.............	26				"
BUTCHER					
Nutzberger, Matthes.......	56	wife	3	18, 12, 7	Luth.
SADDLER					
Weisgerber, John..........	45	wife			Cath.
FIGUREMAKER					
Zerbst, Philip.............	25				Luth.
LOCKSMITH					
Schoenwolf, John..........	23				Ref.
BRICKMAKERS					
Wirs, Frederick............	39	wife		8, 6, 2	Luth.
Meyer, Henry.............	43	"	4	6	Ref.
Pitty, Jacob...............	50			18, 10	"

NAME	AGE	WIFE	SONS	DAUS.	CHURCH
HERDSMAN					
Meyer, Henry.............	31	wife	7, 4, 2		Cath.
SURGEON					
Gudi, Philip..............	40	wife		3, 1	Cath.
MILLERS					
Berchtold, Jacob..........	44	wife	18, 15, 12	4	Ref.
Mueller, Peter............	45	"	15, 14, 7	19, 3	"
Jager, Carl...............	36	"	7	4	"
Schnick, Michel..........	22				Luth.
Cobel, Jacob..............	27	wife	½		Cath.
Shaeflin, Henry...........	49	"	15		"
Walraf, William..........	23				"
Dunckel, Andreas..........	38	wife	3	8, 1	"
Dunckel, John.............	26				"
Martin, Peter.............	33	wife	1	7	"
WIDOWS					
Tieffenbach, Anna........	74				Ref.
Breien, Barba.............	40		18	12, 4	"
Sheffen, Elbot.............	40		10	5	Luth.
Schmidin, Gertrud........	30			3	Cath.
Osevald, Adelia...........	28		8		"
Daubin, Barba............	60				Luth.
Kochin, Elizabeth.........	55				"
Seibelin, Christina........	56				Ref.
Weisrockin, Catherine.....	47			18	"
Baum, Sarah..............	70				"
Crausin, Catherine........	52			24, 16	"
Blasig, Maria.............	46		26		Cath.
Segbin, Apollonia.........	50		24, 18, 9		"
Ganglof, Magdalena.......	60				Luth.
Creuzin, Elizabeth........	48		16, 13	19,17, 11,8	"
Hibig, Anne..............	50		29, 24, 22	26	Ref.
Vogt, Elizabeth...........	48				Cath.
Lisin, Eva................	45		12	10	Ref.
Hilles, Catherine..........	28			2	"
Clossmannin, Margaretha...	40			19	Cath.
Albin, Engel..............	63				Luth.
Reichman, Anne..........	43		9	6, 3	Cath.
UNMARRIED WOMEN					
Khidy, Catherine..........	30				Ref.
Wilhelm, Jane............	28				"
Krutsch, Margaretha.......	24				Cath.
Hausen, Eva..............	24				"
Bork, Elizabeth...........	20				"
Hofman, Sophia...........	18				Luth.
La Force, Barbara........	20				Cath.
La Force, Anne..........	18				"
Bauman, Mary............	30				Luth.
Singerin, Anne............	20				"
Schinkin, Christina.	24				"
Schaeds, Anne............	20				Ref.
Mussel, Barba.............	24				Luth.
Dumbacher, Catherine.....	20				Ref.
Schreibin, Margaretha......	24				Cath.
Heins, Eva......	24				Luth.
Barbe, Anne..............	22				Ref.
Leich, Catherine.....	30				Luth.

NAME	AGE	WIFE	SONS	DAUS.	CHURCH
Schellin, Magdalene........	22				Ref.
Krinin, Mary..............	24				Luth.
Meyerin, Delia............	21				Cath.
Jakoettin, Mary...........	24				Ref.
Jackoettin, Anne..........	20				"
Mosenheim, Mary..........	23				Luth.
Meyerin, Margretha........	23				Ref.
Wagnerin, Catherine.......	20				Cath.
Haasin, Engel.............	22				"
Wiedmacher, Catherine....	24				Ref.

(Endorsed) Miscellanies List of Poor Palatines arrived from Germany the 11th June, 1709. Received from Mr. Ruperti, June 21, 1709. D. 69.

An abstract of the fourth list of 1745 Palatines that are arrived the 11th June, 1709.

> Men................................... 338
> Wives................................ 331
> Widows.............................. 16
> Unmarried Men...................... 92
> Unmarried Women................... 29
> Sons above 14 years.................. 122
> Daughters above 14 years............. 127
> Sons under 14 years.................. 351
> Daughters under 14 years............. 339
>
> ──────
> 1745

An abstract of the three former lists of 4775 Poor Palatines that are come over from Germany from 1st of May to the 10th of June.

> Men................................... 940
> Wives................................ 903
> Widows.............................. 73
> Unmarried Men...................... 292
> Unmarried Women................... 77
> Sons above 14 years................. 257
> Sons under 14 years................. 1016
> Daughters above 14 years............. 247
> Daughters under 14 years..... 970
>
> ──────
> 4775
> The whole sum from 4th list........... 1745
>
> ──────
> All that are here now................. 6520

(Endorsed) Abstract of the lists of the poor German arrived here from the Palatinate from the 1st of May to 11th instant amounting in all to 6520.

Received from Mr. Tribbeko.

Received 16th June, read 21st. D. 70.